urban survival

"**Whether it's on a street or professional level, the most important ingredient of survival is attitude. Get your mind right, then show and prove!**"

DJ Amber

urban survival

the essential guide to street culture

Chrysalis
Impact

First published in 2003 by Chrysalis Impact,
An imprint of Chrysalis Books plc
The Chrysalis Building
Bramley Road
London W10 6SP
United Kingdom

A member of **Chrysalis** Books plc

ISBN 1 84411 015 X

Credits
Commissioning editors: Will Steeds, Chris Stone
Colour reproduction: The Berkeley Square Partnership
Printed and bound in Italy

Dedication
This book is dedicated to Leon 'The FatBloke'
Dawkins (R.I.P) and my son Bailey Leon Johnson.

contents

acknowledgements

Mary Johnson, "Mrs" ArtJaz

If I was the coffee morning or dinner party type, I'd be in my element right now. Look at me – married to a published author, no less. But I've got nowhere to show off about my husband. Mind you, they know all about him in my local shop and takeaway, and my health visitor is waiting with baited breath for the book's release. Not all that "street" at the moment, I'm afraid.

Having Ju working at home kept me company, even though he was often almost insane with deadline pressure. We'd both be up at 4am: me feeding the baby and him writing some mad sh** about "collectable miniature biker's heads". We'd still be up at 6am: me feeding and Ju (still) laughing for no obvious reason.

Did I ever worry that I'd married the wrong guy? Not really. The bit about the guy who wears his tracksuit one leg rolled up because of "a particularly weepy patch of eczema" was my idea. I think we've got more in common than I like to admit. The truth is Julian is incredibly talented. A bit silly – but very talented. You don't have to be his wife to see that.

He writes and draws about what he knows. This book is called Urban Survival and it will help our new family survive for a little while.

Enjoy, and Julian – I'm proud to be your "Mrs" ... X.

Julian ArtJaz

It's been a mad 12 months. About a year ago, the idea of Urban Survival was born. Towards the end of May 2002 my closest mate Leon passed away, 11 days before his 30th birthday. Four weeks later I got married, and on 10 November 2002 my son Bailey was born. Never done a book before. Never had a kid before. No idea how knackered I was going to be. The stress of the amount of work still ahead of me, little one screaming, the wife being physically drained – thought it would never end. It's gotten easier. I just wish the FatBloke was here to keep up the tomfoolery. I'm keeping that Barbecue Kings torch burning for a while, believe.

Special thanks to all the peeps who have contributed to this Fruit Punch. Though I sit constantly in my lab going mad, there's always help at hand: Mary & Bailey; our families: the Johnsons, Higgses and Edwardses (Anne and John – thanks for the babysitting cover); Delores & Natasha; Don aka Dark Bagel; Rob Davy aka Bobby Ewing; Kris Bones; Skymonkey; Tee; Chin; Nobby; Rob @ Protean; Maxi Jazz; Boogie; Soliheen; Joker Starr; Oko; Chris; Gil; Dave Angel; Cyd; Aki; Mis-teeq; Steve Hogan; DJ Amber; Shortee Blitz; Ty; Rodney P; Sweetie Irie; Trish @ Meanwhile; DJ EZ; Dallas @ Skratch; Alfie D; Flowerz; Eddie Otchere; CJ, Jaimie D'Cruz; Will Hobson; Leke @ Aerosoul; Matt @ RWD Magazine; Sticky; Clayton @ TOV; Kenton @ Kaizen; Jennie Baptiste; Mat C; Johnnie Rogue; DJ Swerve; Emma Feline; Elle J Small; Oris Jay; DJ 279; Jay the Doorman.

foreword

Check this out! It's Saturday night. You've gone over your Classics with the toothbrush, got your phone, your scooter key, your "lyrics", a liberal coating of the expensive duty-free aftershave. So get your coat and you're sorted, right?

Ah, but is the phone invisible to the naked eye? Could the whole of your crew fit in your jeans (held in place by a belt round your ankles)? Can you hold raves in your turn-ups? Do you want to queue for your coat at the cloakroom for the rest of your life? Is that moustache even straight? And why are you going out tonight anyway? Don't you know Thursday's the new Saturday?

See? A minefield, and you haven't even left the house.

introduction

Pity our hero, 14-year-old Woodrow Bacon from Little Sticks, Bushes.

Woodrow, a clean-living lad, lived in the country with his grandmother. Life was quite simple and straightforward. An only child, he got up at dawn to do his paper round, then went to school in the village. The school had about 120 pupils in total; they wore uniform, they played sports on acres of private grassland – you get the picture.

Then he would come home, help his gran with chores, do his homework. When that was finished, he sometimes treated himself to a bit of telly. More often, though, his gran requested his company for clarinet practice (she had played years ago, and had been teaching Woodrow for a while now). After a couple of hours he was always ready to hit the sack. Next morning, it was off to school as usual.

One morning, Gran got the first post: there was a letter from the school.

"Eh? What's that boy been up to? He's never had a letter from school before. Wonder what it's about…"

Woodrow & Gran – live from the day's hot topic…

"Dear Mrs Bacon,

I am writing to inform you that your grandson Woodrow has been chosen for an exciting opportunity, to be one of our next batch of exchange students. Due to lack of funds, we will not be partaking in the usual exchange to Switzerland. However, we did not want to disappoint the children and have come up with this last-minute solution. Despite recent OFSTED reports, we understand that the Brother Banton School for Boys is ironing out its problems and offers the ideal opportunity for our boys to experience city life first hand. A suitably accommodating family has been selected with whom Woodrow will spend the week whilst their son, Ricky, will stay here in the village, in your care.

We feel your grandson is an exemplary pupil, and trust that you both will benefit from this exercise. We would like to take this opportunity to congratulate

Woodrow, and to reassure you that the pupils visiting us will be of the same high calibre.

Yours sincerely,

Mr Grantham Peeps

Headteacher

Little Sticks Base Principal Secondary School for Boys."

Gran was excited. "Oo-er! That sounds like fun. Pack your bags, Woody… you're off on an adventure!"

There were four other boys in the exchange programme; they weren't from his year, so he didn't know any of them well enough for chit-chat. Being a little shy, he got comfortable at the back of the carriage and pondered on the trip ahead. He'd never been this far away from home before; he wondered what the big city was really like…

After a pork pie, an apple and a snooze… a couple of sandwiches, another snooze and a chapter of his book, Woodrow's train finally rumbled into the station.

The effect of the city on Woodrow was immediate. Even before he had made it to the Brother Banton School minibus, which had been provided to take him to the suitably accommodating family, he was amazed by how diverse, glamorous and strange it all was. All those new and exciting friends to be made.

Arriving at the Brother Banton School, Woodrow saw that a small group of people had gathered to welcome the exchange students; they turned out to be the host families. After the formal introductions and usual pleasantries, each boy was nudged towards a family and, as it was getting quite late, they were encouraged to make their way back to their cars (just to be on the safe side, as the car park was not very well lit). Woodrow looked puzzled; the headmaster, Mr Wiley, seemed to have forgotten about him.

"Excuse me, sir, am I going home with you?"

"Ah… you must be Woodrow. Erm… yes. We have a lovely family waiting for you, young man. I'll be dropping you off just as soon as we finish here."

When he arrived at what was to be his home for the next seven days, he was taken aback by how relaxed his hosts were about his arrival; anyway it had been a long day, and Woodrow was looking forward to a nice dinner and an early night. He could start his adventures the following day.

Early the next morning, Woodrow popped out for something to eat because he didn't fancy the reheated Chinese takeaway that was the alternative, but trouble was lurking… No sooner had Woodrow turned the corner of the street, than he was confronted by a group of people whom he had never seen the like of before, but was to see plenty more of in the coming days.

Woodrow wasn't used to situations like this. If he'd been street-wise, this is what he could have said or done:

A. "Listen, the Feds are watching us right now – if you still want the stuff we gonna have to do this somewhere else…"

B. "Could I have you guys for dinner in my basement? I'm RAVENOUS!"

C. "Do any of you know where I could bun this chalice?" …or

D. Just aim high; attempt the 40-second mile.

Unfortunately, he didn't; in fact it was to be a while before he learned such subtleties. The closest he'd come to an encounter like this was when he was trapped by the gate in the lower field by some of Farmer Dawkin's cows. That had been very scary, but he soon realised this was more serious. Unsure of what to do he just stood there – paralysed by a combination of fear and ignorance.

Fortunately for him, help was at hand. The mysterious figure who had witnessed Woodrow's arrival at the train station the previous day was watching from afar in his MkII Golf.

Enter Dr Grey, the street culture guru, to guide Woodrow through the minefield that is ...

ANY BIG CITY.

Dr Grey had suspected foul play wasn't too far away; this guy was an old hand… he'd seen it enough times; the local vulture-like petty thugs preying upon any opening conveniently labelled as Easy Pickings. Well, not today…

Suddenly, the attention of the mob turned immediately to the left; one thing was clear – whoever this person was coming towards them, everyone obviously knew of him and hesitantly backed away from Woodrow, who was going through a rollercoaster of emotions at the time. The Doc made his presence felt; he stared directly into the faces of the gang… one after the other, through his jet-black shades – his body language spoke volumes. A few "vulture" eyes looked away or at the floor, unable to match the intensity of the eye-to-eye challenge; the others just frowned, having lost out on "some good eating"…

COME WITH ME IF YOU WANT TO LIVE.

I'LL EXPLAIN LATER.

Woodrow was extremely grateful for the help of this mysterious fellow, and his words of wisdom. Without his intervention Woodrow might have been robbed – or even worse. But, just as he was preparing to thank his rescuer, Dr Grey vanished, almost as quickly as he had appeared.

Reflecting later on his experiences, Woodrow concluded that it had been a very harrowing day. The "suitably accomodating" family didn't seem to be at all bothered what happened to him and, disillusioned by talk of "family" and "character building", Woodrow was beginning to conclude that this exchange programme had gone all wrong for him.

"Will I even survive the week?" he wondered.

Fortunately for Woodrow, his Guardian Angel had not disappeared for good. Dr Grey was poised to return and, under his guidance, Woodrow was about to experience a week that would change his life for ever.

chapter 1
the characters

"I knew these two geezers, their AKAs were Agony and Damage. I never asked why 'cos I didn't want them to show me, and their only words were 'Mmm' and 'Ya'man'."

Gil, photographer

YOU ARE IN SERIOUS NEED OF SOME ASSISTANCE, KID. YOU **HAVE** TO KNOW WHO TO SIDE WITH AND WHO TO AVOID. HERE'S A ROUGH CROSS-SECTION OF THE URBAN COMMUNITY.

BLUE CHEESE!

dr grey

Well, first there's me. I like to think of myself as: The Tour Guide, The Sherpa, The Agony Aunt; The Lifesaver, The Coastguard, The Swimming Pool Attendant; The Fixer, The Cleaner, The Equalizer.

Remember judging books by covers?

Occasionally, and when you're least expecting it, your bacon will be saved by the most unlikely of sources. You're adamant that you've really upset someone this time and you have earned yourself a serious kicking – "No getting out of this one" – when, out of nowhere, a complete stranger shows up and appears to put himself in the firing line – sticks his neck out for you. I am that guy.

I watched the situation unfold and thought to myself, "I could sit here and watch nature take its course, or I could put down my sandwich and actually make a difference, change the outcome of the game. Yeah, why not?"

Then not only do I give you advice on the quickest and safest way off this patch, but I nonchalantly offer tips & advice (free of charge) on how to improve your chances of hassle-free existence in the big city.

WATCH YOUR
BACK, SON.

the bouncer

Usually found in pairs, most of them fit into two categories: Big or Small. Tell-tale characteristics:

Big: Over 6ft 6 tall * Ridiculously heavy build * Large head * Deep voice

Small: Under 6ft tall * Lean, wiry build * Small head * Weasel-like features, scary eyes

Basically, if you have to get on the wrong side of one, make sure it's one of the Big variety. Quite simply, you can easily outrun them, due to their "large herbivore" bulk; whereas the Small bouncer will chase you over that wall, under that car. He'll find you; that's what he does; that's ALL he does.

the drug dealer

As you may discover, there is no particular "look" for a drug dealer. You might think, "long mac, loads of pockets inside, bit like a sweet shop, dirty-looking, bit like a flasher". Scratch that thought. Male, female, black, white, yellow, red, brown, green – doesn't matter. No rules. Any and everybody could technically be on a "hustle", for one reason or another.

So here's a generalized profile of a succeesful pusher, who seems to be doing quite well out of his "job": owner of many mobile phones, each one rings with orders from a specific "bracket" of clients (which dictates what car to drive to make the drop-off); keys to two or more flash cars, lives at home with mum (who is regularly showered with gifts and fabricated stories about his "promotion" – she's so proud); rents a "slaughterhouse" (place to keep stock); works odd hours; and claims to be a jeweller if stopped and questioned (hence the digital scales, loads of gold and stacks of cashflow).

the clubber

Accountant by day, works long hours in a stuffy office, for a boss who doesn't seem to know the difference between work and pleasure; boring himself to tears with talk of stocks and shares, banks and bonds. Our young employee watches the clock; thinking to himself, "Come on 5 o'clock, come on!" As soon as the big hand hits the 12, he's out the door.

"Mr Peevley? I'll have those things on your desk first thing Monday morning."

On the way home.

"Dave, Can you hear me? Gotta talk fast 'cos we're just about to go through a tunnel. Meet me in the bar about nine. We'll get bevvied up first, then we'll hit the club. Alright mate, see you then."

Outside the club, distinct whiff of alcohol on breath, will stand in freezing queue for hours and pay full (extortionate) entry fee. Luminous plastic jewellery-wearing, pill-popping, "I-Love-You-Man"-declaring.

The Everyday Raver: similar but works in entertainment; working hours are more flexible so can literally rave night after night, in the name of 'research'."

> **"Party-people, and that goes out especially to all you who think you're in the know, the only thing you need to recognize is that sometimes you have to contribute a few shekels, if only to help out those who are hard at work trying to entertain you. It may be cool to be on the guestlist all the time, but we all have bills to pay. Hmmm."**
>
> Alfie, journalist and promoter

the ligger

The premier blagger of entrance to all clubs, industry shindigs, PTA wine & cheese buffets, whatever – doesn't matter. Always claims to know the DJ, be the DJ's girlfriend/wife or be part of the promotion team, sponsors, etc. "Do you know who I am? Who d'you think provided those balloons?!!" Works in music/PR/fashion/press, hence the extensive knowledge of what parties and where, and whose guestlist can be exploited.

Phrases include: "Are those the free cocktails? I'll have 12 of them ferried over to my table in the corner" and "You've got me mixed up with someone else, let me see that guestlist – give it here! Let... Go of it! Oi!!"

SORRY, I DON'T PAY.

the dj

This is your job, your career. You work nights, you sleep in the day, answering your many messages when you wake up at 5.30pm.

The obsession of having your whole house decorated in vinyl.

"What do I need a wife and kids for? This is my baby right here, all I care about is my vinyl, geez!"

Every day the postman brings more 12-inch square brown envelopes to the door, then down to the local depot for pick-up: freebies that couldn't fit through the letterbox. Acetates, dub plates, passes, comps. The Ligger Supreme. You don't pay. For anything.

You're playing at some swanky house party tonight. Some rich bird with dosh wants you to play an all-night set for her birthday, no worries. As long as they keep me sweet, I'm all theirs. What shall I wear? Fisherman hat, jeans. Does this shirt smell? Nah, it's alright, one more wear won't hurt. These boots ain't too muddy. Yep, two squirts of the old Buffalo Juice. Audi keys, record box, ciggies, Palm Pilot. Let's go. Get to the party. Some plum opens the door, looking at you like, "Er – can I help you?"

"I'm the DJ, ain't I?"

the city slicker

The Pinstripe Suit, very astute. The flash car keys are blatantly visible on the restaurant table, latest mobile and personal organizer only a blink away.

Lunchtime: orders pricey steaks and seafood, takes immense pride in knowledge of the most swanky eateries. "Only the Best for my lads," he declares drunkenly, whilst ordering the sixth bottle of plonk. Always pissed outside the pub after work, being proper leery, showing the pure extent of his immaturity. He's a laugh but just doesn't know how to act in social situations, especially when there's "alky-hol" involved.

May be a Class "A" drug user. Thinks he and his dealer are best mates. That, in turn, makes him cool because he has one cool "ghetto" mate. His peers are impressed at the "authenticity" of his urban connections.

the cabbie

Has that "Del Boy" look: flat cap, comfy sweater, slacks and chunky gold watch. Suffers from chronic verbal diarrhoea, "You know who I had in my cab last night?" Actually, they can't be faulted on their proper knowledge of how to get around town. "Have you seen the amount of streets there are in London? Not for the faint-hearted, this job."

Rogue minicabbie

Proper shifty-looking, may have omitted personal hygiene and shaving from the list of Cabbie Priorities. Quite opportunistic when it comes to determining a fare, knowing you're more than likely plastered and will do anything to get home to bed. Drives a noisy, barely-road-legal old banger – how it got through the MOT is anyone's guess. The chances are that he hasn't had a chance to stop for lunch today, so will be hurriedly munching his way through an overcooked carcass of some description (while you're haggling over routes and fares you'll have caught a fair bit of meat scraps in the face due to the intensity of the bartering). Half-empty "Krazy Fried Chicken" boxes in the footwell, the car's in desperate need of a few Magic Tree air fresheners, that's for sure. Don't worry, all being well you'll be home soon. Concentrate on that image.

the Footy Fan

Used to be seen as just a thug, a hooligan, and you'd only be seen scrapping in your own locality; whereas today's supporters wear slick designer gear. Organized fights are communicated by text messaging; and all have respectable city jobs – lawyers, doctors, stockbrokers, etc.

Still be very wary of matchdays, and where the stadiums are – north, east, south, west. You might be on the Underground going about your merry way, and just happen to be wearing that replica football shirt you were given as a present. Of course you're going to wear it with pride; how are you to know that team had, only this evening, been involved in a heated Derby and won after a 90-minute Gladiatoresque epic? And there you are, only two stops away from copping a terrible beating in the last carriage, because of your callous incitement of the disbelieving supporters.

"What's this guy ON? You must be taking the p*."**

the trendy b-boy

Outfitted from head to toe in nothing but imported & exclusive US gear. Has a different sports outfit for each day, to emulate their Favourite Rap artist.

Wears a fisherman hat (with the tiniest label to identify urban fashion house) but doesn't fish (would faint whilst putting the worm on the hook). Never been hiking in his life, but owns an impressive selection of "high-end" mountain walking boots (with not a scrap of mud in the tread); basketball boots?; sweatbands & tennis shoes (tennis – what?); running shoes (run – what?); never been yachting, but owns a good few designer showerproof jacket and trouser suits; doesn't play golf yet lives in colourful golfing flat caps. Multi-layered goose-down polar expedition parka, anyone?

the bashment girls

Shiny Everything.

Hairstyles: Finger-waves, coloured – especially green, blue or red; jheri-curls, wigs and weaves of all colours, styles and textures.

Jewellery: A whole heap of gold rings (at least two on each finger), sovereigns galore; nose and ear studs – shapes vary widely from marijuana leaf, sport brand logo, to pistol. Upper lip stud (beauty spot-style). Very big gold earrings (hoops big enough to fit around other body parts) and tiaras. And gold teeth – "fronts" and caps. Highly-decorated nail extensions, "with Diamonique!"

Clothing: Leggings with bits missing; fishnet and lace tights; "batty riders" or half-bottom shorts; lingerie; "desert" boots; different-coloured fake fur outfits; jewelled, feathered (or both) clothing (beware of shedding fur or lost jewels); stiletto-heeled sandals with the laced-up leg.

Make no mistake, they make an intimidating prospect for anyone bar the most thick-skinned or heartless guy. Infinitely louder than the male equivalent. Tread carefully.

the Fashion crew

Hail mainly from West London, more recently East Central London (i.e. Hoxton); garms are so exclusive, you need special passes and a season membership to enter the boudoirs; elitist outlets, haute couture.

In fact, so designer they're completely devoid of labels. You can't tell whether the piece of clothing cost 50p from a charity shop or £600 from a well-respected designer's rare auction. They have real hatred of the fashion victims who wear logos and brand names to show their sources.

You know the type: the Fin hairstyle (bleached at the top); "Chips"-style aviator sunglasses; sleeveless T-shirts with distressed Japanese prints; or old-skool "Retro" tracksuit tops with the neck zipped right up; twisted jeans (or whatever the latest "cut" is); space-age, skinny-fit running shoes (with the cloven hoof) or '70s reissued plimsolls; one-shoulder rucksack for carrying gadgets and bottled water, healing crystals and an apple.

the uhg champagne set

"Bling bling" suits this crowd perfectly. Dancing with champagne bottles in the air (randomly pouring out bubbly on the floor), ice buckets and plastic champagne flutes, due to the "No Glass" policy, which stemmed from fights getting out of hand far too regularly. "No baseball caps, no trainers, CCTV in operation" seems out of place when you see the Bugsy Malonesque suited-up party-goers. (I could never quite get my head around dressing up to the nines, just to "bug out" on the dancefloor, sweating your clothes right through to the skin. Dry cleaners must be making an absolute killing.)

Phrase: "BOOOOOOOOOOO!", which replaced "REWIND!!" as the response to a favourable record that needed to be "wheeled" back to the start before everybody in the place went nuts. Initially, you may not comprehend what the crowd are thinking if you're new to this.

"Eh? But I thought it was quite good, why are they booing?"

the rudeboy

The Roughneck; The Raggamuffin; the Ghetto Yoot. One of the most abrasive of the lineup (probably second only to the Baked Bean Mum), always travels as part of a pack, rarely is one seen on his own. They are the Angry Bees; disturb the nest at your own risk.

On their tiny mobiles, on mopeds, on BMXs, bandana'd up, hair canerowed down or fully-blown-Afroed out (Afro Pick in hair), coloured drainpipe jeans, hoodies and scowls. They adhere to their own in communication; on one scam or another, fast-talking makes it difficult for outsiders to comprehend their vocal interplay (this must be a survival technique, which has proved successful as their numbers have swelled a hundredfold in recent years).

Commonly found taking over and establishing new territory, body language shows aggressive posturing in defence of the new spot, wherever it may be: congregated on buses (upstairs at the back); mock-fighting on the trains (this always looks worse than it actually is – an intimidatory display used to unnerve potential enemies); in mobile phone shops – in the process of getting kitted out or topped up; or at funfairs (only on the bumper cars).

Most likely to be singled out or targeted for scrutiny because of their volatile nature. In summary, best to avoid.

the skater

You might think that if you've seen one skater, you've seen them all, when really there's a wide range of skater categories most people are unaware of. You can begin with the main difference – between the new and the old. The more trendy skater has kitted himself out in the newest and freshest gear: brand new imported jeans with visibly sharp ironed creases. He is in it for the look and is never the first to be testing out his physical prowess on the tarmac, in full view of onlookers. Yeah, they can flick the board off the floor into their hands, but what else? We need to know. Always seen in the CD bar or Internet café (too many distractions, so many ways to use your sunny Saturday afternoons).

Then there's the rough-looking skater: more grungey, long chain hanging from oversized, faded flared jeans, with holes torn in the lower leg. He's in it for the feel and the thrill, not so concerned with the latest fashions. He's more interested in the latest tricks and actually pulling them off, instead of just being able to identify and quote them.

the crusty

Gaunt, angry-looking, dyed matty dreads, always in a band, plays guitar or mouth organ, maybe has a skinny mongrel with a blue rope lead and dirty bandana tied round its neck. Has old blueish tattoos on his hands and neck, unwanted remnants of an even angrier teenage existence. Hangs out with old rastas and brings them cans of strong beer as presents, to keep them sweet for when he needs to beg a (weed-related) favour.

Don't get into any heated politcal discussion with them unless you know your onions – these guys know all about homeless rights, squatter's rights, council issues, who runs the local constituency and why you'd be wasting your time asking for their assistance with anything because "they don't understand us, or what we have to put up with".

Lives on canned goods, and whatever dole money the state says they're entitled to (which is never enough, I know – I've been there). When between squats, they'll be found sleeping in their mate's Transit (van, the one with the curtains in the Superstore car park).

the tagger

Typically of school age, has an in-depth knowledge of permanent and waterproof marker pens: the makes, the types of nib (bullet-point, chisel, etc.). Not necessarily a graffiti writer, or even any good at art, but likes the idea of getting "up": having their "tag" visible to other taggers in every corner of the city (or as far as you can get in any one day with an All-Zones Travelcard). They weigh up the priorities: between a double period of Science and going tagging to get your name "all-city", they're skipping school.

More recently, the introduction of keys and other sharp instruments as a tagging medium has become increasingly widespread, making the "public" (adult population) more aware of the damage caused to property, especially on bus and train windows. Therefore the penalties for being caught in the act have risen sharply as a response and deterrent (personally I would have thought the possibility of falling off a railway bridge onto live electric rails or into tightly-coiled barbed wire would have been deterrent enough). Still, boys will be boys, and at that age it's easy to see yourself as indestructible:

"It'll NEVER happen to me, mate."

the baked beans

Dad "works" down the bookies, dresses in worn-out jeans with no belt; baggy, off-white vest indoors; Christmas-type jumpers and white trainers outdoors; smells a bit "drinky-drinky". Mum chain-smokes, does the odd shift on the tills in the local supermarket (not the Superstore but the single till with no scanner, only two hand baskets and one of the handles is broken, no-automatic-doors shop); wears flesh-coloured leggings and mansize dayglo T-shirts, dreams of a holiday romance with Magnum in Tenerife.

The kids: You can never tell what they're wearing or even IF they're wearing clothes, as they move too fast for the human eye to see, buzzing on sweet drinks and chews. At school they have to stick together, because their family's obvious financial status has left them open to relentless playground taunts. They never really get it bad though because of their mother's ferocious temper, which the whole school knows about, including the teachers – they're not immune. This woman will blow her top at the drop of a hat, believe. Best to avoid.

woody bacon

The human guinea pig for our experiment: The Geek; The Patsy; The Fall Guy; The Hero of the Hour. He's the guy looking confused, holding onto the map, looking for streetnames and signposts. The guy at the train station on his own, pulling heavy suitcases or lugging a rucksack that's twice as tall as him over his knackered shoulders. Who gets on the Tube and is dying to sit down, but he can't because someone's got their feet up on the only spare seat and isn't prepared to negotiate over who needs it more.

This could be you.

If you've come to town as a tourist, or to visit family and they're not really streetwise; not particularly into the idea of dragging you around dimly-lit estates after dark just so you can say you know about "urban life", you could so easily fall foul of any "Road Code" that your tour operator or even your gran didn't know to warn you about.

You wonder, "Where are the manners? What happened to common decency? Saying please and thank you? Opening doors for ladies and having respect for your elders?" These things do still exist, but for so many people they're just not that important any more. It would be pointless to expect these basic gestures from everyone. That's why it's such a novelty to witness any of these old-fashioned niceties.

chapter 2
fashion

"Street culture and fashion breeds originality filtered by mainstream culture. Body language, fashion and dance has its own code within street culture: either you're in or..."

Jennie Baptiste, photographer

trainers

As you can tell from all the other street cats on your travels, it is imperative that you make an impression, a good impression (or at least bad, meaning good). Kids can be cruel. Remember going back to school after the summer holiday, assuming that as you've deliberately torn the toe off your old, name-brand trainers, your parents will upgrade to the latest model? Surely.

"No? Okay then, last season's model. I'm sure the gang won't disown me. Wait a minute – Mum! We've just passed the sports shop. Where are you going? Mum, that's the wrong shop. What you doing? Mum? MUM!!"

You drag yourself slowly out of the bargain basement of the cheap shoe shop, about 20 paces behind your mother and little sister, who is marginally too young to be affected by the trends which govern your life so strictly. So she sniggers at your misfortune.

Don't worry, she'll be going through the same thing this time next year.

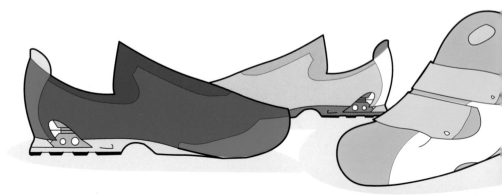

Obviously, to be seen to be "on point", you absolutely must be in some "now" stuff – not yesterday's but Today's Press. Most essentially, this must cost in excess of £100, no matter how ugly it looks. Leave the price tag on if you have to – the public must be informed of how "jiggy" you are.

Some will try a new thing, no matter what it is. You've seen this type of footwear. In the past you may have thought, "Why, they're just slippers for spacemen, kung fu teachers, ballet dancers and ninjas", but no, they are widely available to pretty much anyone. Word of advice: they do come with special socks. Not many people can go barefoot in trainers for more than 40 seconds without stirring the sweaty beast – it's not personal; it's chemical.

If you don't want your name to be mentioned in hushed tones, take sensible precautions to avoid that "citrus funk":

1 Check out the latest urban magazines, featuring today's hippest hip-hop and R&B stars, who get paid significant wedge by sportswear giants to prance about in their clobber.

2 The more technologically advanced the materials involved, the better. Look for some super-light Gore-Tex, nu-buck, kevlar uppers, kryptonite, etc.

3 Forget about any "old skool trainers" talk – that's old people talk.

Okay, you're in the West End, in the brand-spanking-new shopping centre, in the multi-million-pound, state-of-the-art sportswear facility, showcasing the latest in hi-tech imported "boxfresh" minty joints and you bring out your manky old, 1970s-era, elastic-front plimsolls, complete with that "worn-in" feel. Questions will be asked; faces will be pulled.

A DAY IN THE LIFE OF A ... trainer freak

For a month you save your pocket money, your wages, your dole, whatever. Your man who works in the sports shop on Saturdays gives you his Spring catalogue (after you threaten to break his arm if he doesn't comply) and tells you what day the next shipment of imports is due. The wait is unbearable. Hope they get here before the weekend of that party, they have to.

It's Friday lunchtime. Your phone vibrates with an incoming message: "THE EAGLE HAS LANDED. GET DOWN TO THE SHOP NOW. THE IMPORTS HAVE ARRIVED!" Your heartbeat goes through the roof. "You guys, catch you later!" Helmet on, moped engine screaming at 39mph – SKREEEECH! Just miss the bollards; park the bike up on the pavement; curious passers-by wonder "Where's the fire?" as you rush through the double glass doors of the sports shop (helmet still on). The two security guards tag-team-up on you with the Flying Clothesline, assuming you're on a smash-'n'-grab raid. How were they to know anything different? After the melee, they dust you down and apologize sincerely – that scuff on your chin will heal soon enough.

Eyes wide, you step to the newly-displayed crop of trainers. You catch the dribble from the corner of your mouth with your shoulder. "Oooh, that new-shoe smell." You slowly reach for the stash of folded cash from your sock and mumble to yourself, "At last – it's Christmas."

trousers

Used to be a male-only domain, but these days a universal staple of the masses in general.

What is unfair is the pressures on women not only to wear the trousers but to possess buttocks pleasing to the eye, because guys will stare or not stare; women will cuss or not cuss. "Where's she going with THAT BOTTOM?! Disgusting."

Also, VPL (Visible Pantie Line) can be a woman's nightmare, especially when she's trying her best to look her best.

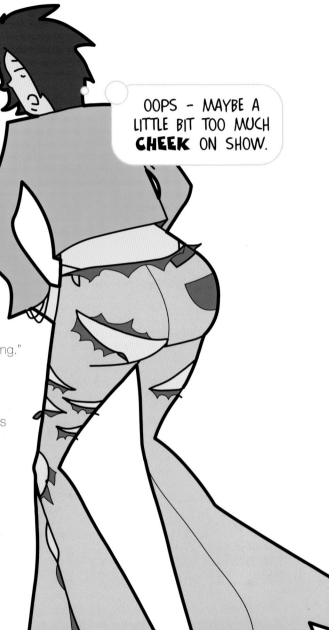

OOPS - MAYBE A LITTLE BIT TOO MUCH **CHEEK** ON SHOW.

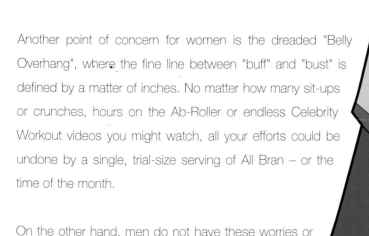

Another point of concern for women is the dreaded "Belly Overhang", where the fine line between "buff" and "bust" is defined by a matter of inches. No matter how many sit-ups or crunches, hours on the Ab-Roller or endless Celebrity Workout videos you might watch, all your efforts could be undone by a single, trial-size serving of All Bran – or the time of the month.

On the other hand, men do not have these worries or concerns. As long as they've got a recognized name brand on show, they can more or less get away with anything (within reason). For instance:

BIG TURN-UPS

There seems to be no limit to how high these go up your leg. I'm sure there are people who abuse this fashion by storing items such as peanuts, chewing gum, pack of hankies or "whacky baccy" in them.

Nudge-nudge, wink-wink.

HOLD ON, MATE.
CAN I HELP YOU?!!

PAY AND DISPLAY
(or Neo-Builder's Bum)

I'm sure that if I'd never seen this unusual display before I wouldn't know what to make of it either, but let me assure you that staring is so not the answer.

It's not clear where this look originated, as the classic "builder's look" does not usually incorporate designer underwear, but like so much of street culture, the youngsters have embraced the idea and taken it a step further (maybe even a step too far). Making it an unquestionable example of "fashion fusion", where the ultimate theme will always be:

"If you've got it, flaunt it." (And if you haven't got it, boldly pretend that you have.)

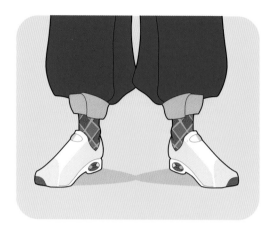

TIGHT ROLL-UPS

This look was adopted by young urban males, which consisted of: incredibly baggy jeans or Jumbo cords, diamond socks and slim-fit "Torsion" trainers.

Extra care was needed in preparation for the "roll-up" stage. First you would take the hem of the jeans, and with one flap, wrap around the ankle, rolling it up or doubling it over, making sure it was tight enough to stay up of its own accord. Then you made sure your diamond socks were pulled up tight (no baggy socks allowed). You found yourself a full-length mirror and, hey presto, your look was complete…

But that wasn't all. You had to be constantly on guard, making sure that your roll-ups hadn't just unrolled themselves when you weren't looking.

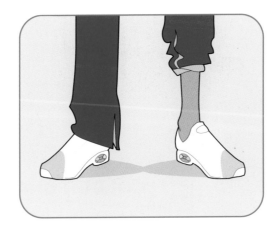

ONE LEG UP

This look seems to have evolved into fashion more recently. The parameters of the style are much more liberal than the Tight Roll-Up; you can include jogging bottoms, "crushed" velour tracksuit bottoms, showerproofs, etc. as well as jeans and cords.

Specific origins of this look: was it the Old English Country Gent Cyclist, with the deerstalker hat, monocle and leather trouser clips (for keeping the hems of his tweed "strides" out of his chain)? Or was it in fact inspired by medical reasons – someone was sent home from the doctors with specific instructions; that their particularly weepy case of eczema on the ankle needed to being sufficiently aerated? Or was it, like in most cases, discovered totally by accident, and one brave soul was brazen enough to "bop" it, and had no idea of the effect it had on the current need for the next lick?

COLOUR CHAOS?

You may have noticed the unusual trouser trend: insanely colourful drainpipe jeans with a metallic finish, favoured by many teenage males from the UK Garage and Ragga crowds.

Big logos: often too big for the garment. Sometimes it seems that as long as everything is name-brand, it can be worn freely without the slightest consideration for acceptable colour co-ordination.

Amongst the styles are: Cuban Sunset, Ibiza Beach Scene, Kenyan Safari, Birds of Paradise, Renaissance Life Painting and Oriental Brass Rubbing.

"When putting outfits together, take careful note of what suits YOU. Don't pick something out purely on the basis that the label says 'Evisu' or 'Moschino'; a name brand does not mean that the garment is automatically gonna look good on you!"

CJ, writer/journalist

hoodies

The Ultimate Thug Item: these should be an essential part of your wardrobe if you mean business when it comes to looking the part. Picture it: you're walking down the street towards one group of heads; on the other side of the road is another group – but without hoodies. Tell me you aren't crossing over as soon as traffic permits – don't lie, I've seen it.

The flipside of this is, no matter WHO you are, once the Hood is up, the clock is ticking. People will avoid eye contact with you; nervous shoppers unable to determine your intentions will alert store managers to your presence; security guards will gather at all available exits. Is attempting to buy your regular copy of the *Angling Times* worth the potential showdown, accusations and inevitable body search?

The choice is yours.

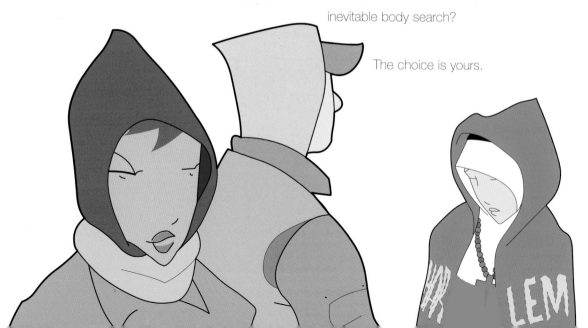

YO, WHAT UP, DAWG?
MY SH*T IS **PROPER**, SON.
I AIN'T **PLAYIN'** KID.
MY GEAR'S **OFF THE HOOK**
THIS YEAR.
YOU **BETTER** RECOGNIZE -
'CAUSE EITHER WAY I AIN'T
HAVIN' IT, Y'HEAR ME?
I WAS **BUILT** FOR THIS,
DAWG...

XXXL THUG STATEMENT

us sports gear

Basketball vests and shorts; baseball and American football shirts; this is one area where oversize is essential. The shirts and long shorts make your skinny forearms and shins look like twigs; the vests double as summer dresses for days on the beach. Official licences and logos: imitations are strictly prohibited. Bright colours so you can be seen in the Carnival crowd.

No I don't understand it either. I watch thugged-out rap dudes on the music television channels on cable TV; broad-shouldered, burly-looking street soldiers posturing Hard with… smiley cartoon animal faces on their chests.

The mixed messages are bewildering.

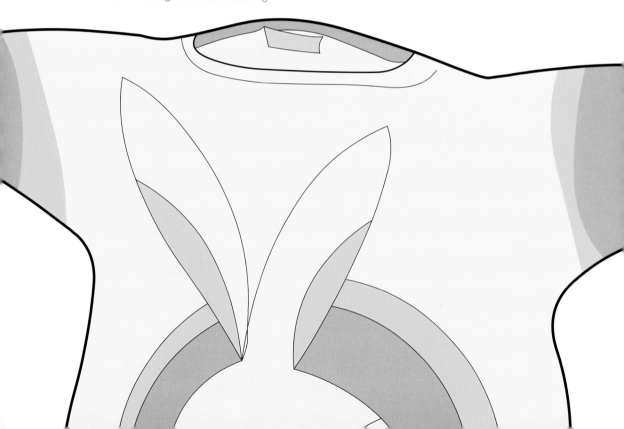

string vests

Worn predominantly by the Ragga crowd. The best place to find them is down the market, in various colours. (Beware, white vests must be washed regularly.) The "stretched-out" look is deliberate. Can either be worn as an undergarment or as outerwear.

WoW (Word of Warning)
Ensure you have a long-sleeved garment of some description to hand; remember, this is not the Caribbean (typical scenario below):

There you are, chilling out at someone's back-garden barbecue on a Sunday afternoon, packed buffet plate slightly folded in your lap. A single cloud passes across the sun and it feels like winter. "Quick, borrow me your Mum's cardigan! I'm FREEZING!!"

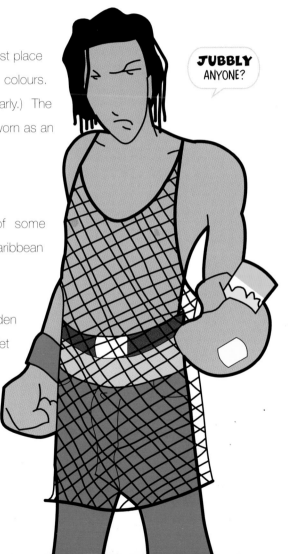

JUBBLY ANYONE?

"You shouldn't really be ashamed to wear a hat if you didn't get your hair plaited in time – Wear Your Hat With Pride! But if it's a 'Hats-Off' night, you're in trouble."

Joker Starr, MC

hairstyles – women

"My special trick in the winter is this: it's cold, but you've just done your hair, so you don't really want to wear a hat, but your ears are really cold – those big DJ headphones make great earmuffs, and you can listen to your favourite tunes at the same time!"

Yvette, Make-Up Artist

What's going on with women's hair these days? Teenage girls (of all nationalities) have the scraped-back ponytail, multi-hair bobble thing going on, with a section of rock-hard gelled fringe stuck onto the forehead. The young(ish) women you see whilst shopping down the local market have the five-layer multicoloured weave that defies gravity. The strategically plaited corn-row styles that you know took all day are only gonna last about a week – if she sleeps in her silk scarf. Did you know about that one? You know when a woman doesn't know about the silk scarf thing, because her hair resembles old candy floss and has a slight browny-ginger tinge going on, when the hair's supposed to be black.

KEEPING IT REAL?

Do you have a Death Wish? Do you want to go back to the House of Pain?

Even if it's blatantly obvious that the hair on her head was not there a few hours ago, there must be easily a million and one OTHER THINGS you could talk about, APART FROM You Know What.

A wise man once said: "Go with your gut instinct. Just say the first thing that comes into your head."

I'm sure that's the same man, still laying face-down in the kerb, with his nose sticking through the back of his hat. All because he didn't know everything…

hairstyles – men

The Fade

The Plaits

The obligatory
Afro Pick

Never has there been such diversity of male hairstyles. Gone are the days of the jheri-curl and the high-top (phew). Today, we've got the little afros; the chiney-bumps; relaxed crop (?!?!); the short back and sides with fade; plaits; skinny dreads; skinheads; afros; and the Hoxton Fin (see below).

But isn't it good that some guys are actually finding styles that suit them and sticking with it, instead of just adopting a 'do only because it's the 'In Thing'"? Just because bald heads are cool doesn't mean Joe Bloggs with the worst head shape you've ever seen (complete with unexplainable craters, gashes and lumps) can get away it.

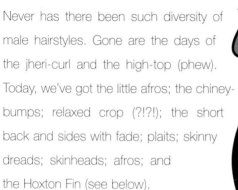

"Growing your hair for the 'In Crowd' or going against the grain, some went too far. If your hair(line) started too far from or too close to your eyes, then the 'Fringe Monitor' would have to visit your brow. Depended on what barber you went to and if he was having a good or a bad day. Maybe making up your own hairline template would save you the embarrassment."

Rob Davy, Mutiny UK

SMASHING.

headwear

THE BASEBALL CAP

Absolutely Priceless. Everyone knows the drill: you have to have not just one but several. At least one per matching outfit (consisting of hat, top, belt, shoes, laces – bandana and detachable mobile phone cover optional).

How to Rock Your Cap

Straight Ahead: The traditional, Safe option; this is how they were made to be worn.

Bent-Round Brim: Takes care and attention (the Urban Standard).

Unbent Brim: You're either Old Bill or Nu-Skool Cool (very recent).

To the Back: Only Official Licensed Fitted Caps. No plastic adjustables, with wayward tuft of hair poking out.

To the Side: 1 o'clock is cool, 3 o'clock – you're too new to this. Chances are, your idea of Urban is "Ice Ice Baby".

An example of a Bent-Round Brim

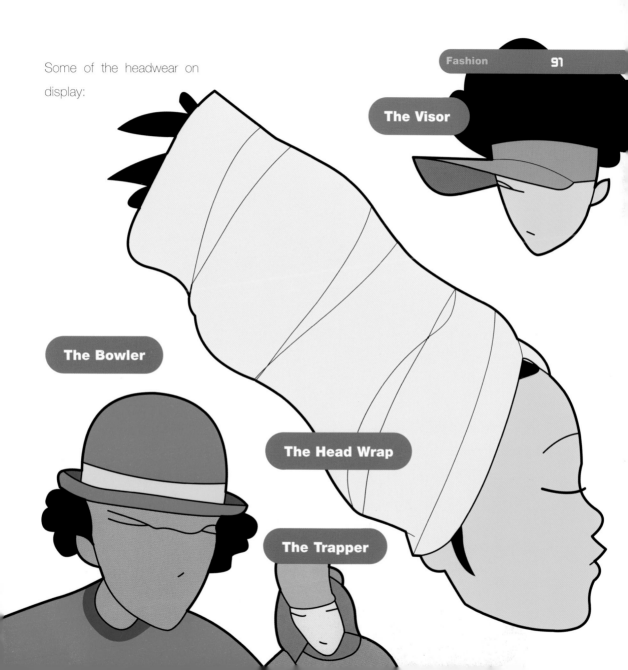

Some of the headwear on display:

The Visor

The Bowler

The Head Wrap

The Trapper

The Doo Rag

The Sock Hat

SOCK HATS & DOO RAGS

The Sock Hat: Obviously originated from the cut-off top ladies' tights, but that doesn't necessarily mean you can go into any haberdashery and purchase "5-pairs-for-the-price-of-4" best thermal, ribbed-cotton hosiery.

The Doo Rag: From a practical point of view, the intended use of this accessory was to assist in the formation of the Sporting Wave (Cab Calloway-style), but also to provide an ideal accompaniment to your matching baseball cap and shirt, trousers and shoes.

BANDANAS

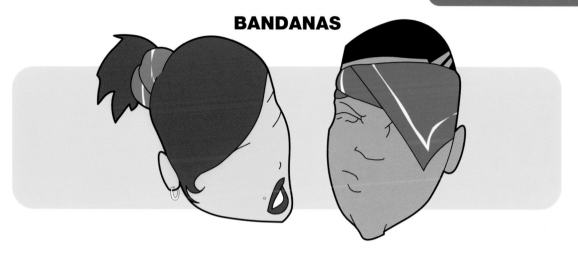

An essential part of any fashion-conscious young person's attire. The infinite range of colours makes it very easy to integrate with any look: as a headscarf (on its own, or in conjunction with a hat or cap), neckerchief, hairband or for just hanging out from the back pocket of your jeans (or even around your ankle, as part of the "one leg up" trouser style).

There is a generalized idea that the colours of your bandana refer to gang culture – "What set you from?". This was true on the West Coast, USA, in the '80s and early '90s, but the same rules don't apply over here (if you see anyone trying to force this on you, they're either stuck in a time warp or just trying it, being opportune).

Go ahead, mix & match to your heart's content. Just remember to wash them from time to time. I'm sure some kids think their rags don't stink.

SUNGLASSES

(even at night)

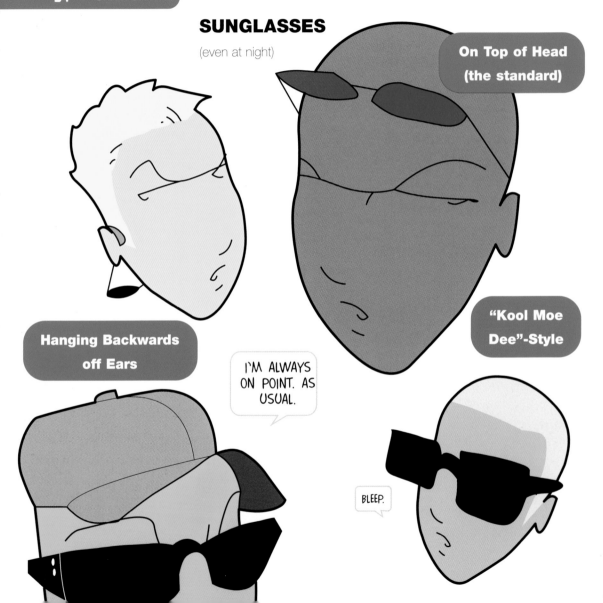

On Top of Head (the standard)

Hanging Backwards off Ears

I'M ALWAYS ON POINT. AS USUAL.

"Kool Moe Dee"-Style

BLEEP.

COLOUR CONTACTS

Who says black people can't have blue eyes and mad people can't have yellow eyes with Smiley faces? Forget rules: if you've got the nerve, you can get the eyes. My only advice is to go for crazy colours. If they look too realistic, it could be a real letdown for any lonely, love-struck fool who was just looking for an excuse. They'll come over to you on the dancefloor, just at that moment when the smoke has finally eaten into the backs of your corneas, and started to burn.

"Your eyes are like reflections of angels, pools of ecstasy, blah blah, waffle, etc."

When actually you would die for some cucumber slices right about now. You've got to nip this in the bud immediately. The only course of action is to gouge the contacts out of your own eyes and show them to the pest. "There!! Are You Bloody Happy Now?!!"

decoration

You may have heard "bling", and not known what the Dickens was going on.

Well "bling" is the norm – he's got it just right; "bling-bling" – he's showing off now; "bling-bling-bling" –.Mr T; "bling" x 4 – Arab Sultan.

You might see a particularly flashy gent and think to yourself, "Wow! He's got to be A Fly Guy," but remember, all that glitters ain't gold.

He might tell you that he's a top-selling recording artist from Greater Peckham, taking a well-deserved lunchbreak from the studio, when in fact it's all a sham.

Don't be fooled. He may simply be a mouthy opportunist, part-time, shelf-stacking East Street Market "Goldidium"-wearing Muppet.

There's also a lot of talk about "Ice" and "Bezel". This is an arena you should only enter if you're making a footballer's wages, to be on the safe side. "White Gold", "Yellow Gold" and "Red Gold"? When you're only familiar with "Green Gold"? Well, that was the colour it was after wearing it for some time. Should it not be called "Gan-Green Gold"?

Let it be told. If you don't own an unusually thick neck with tough skin, please beware The Rash – hundreds of tiny golden flakes of metal embedded in your dermis: open sores, left untreated. Don't leave it until it's too late, or it'll be a lifetime of itchy scarves and polo-necks.

I PITY THE FOOL.

PROTECT YOUR NECK. FULL STOP.

NAILS

"This girlfriend of mine goes to the nail parlour what seems like every day. It looks as if she single-handedly keeps those staff in business."

Cyd, Clubber

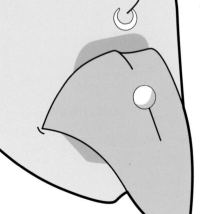

TATTOOS AND PIERCING

You may have thought that body piercing and tattoos were the pastime of punks, squaddies and circus freaks, but that's all changed in recent years. No one knows for sure why, but I assume it's been the merging of subcultures and musical tastes. Out on the dancefloor, ladies display pierced belly buttons and tongues, and cute shoulder tats.

But like everything else, know when to stop/what looks good. Keep your "body bling" clean; swellings and pus are not a pretty sight.

Where the "Hellraiser" look works and even helps while in college, once you're in the working world, looking like a pincushion has its drawbacks when applying for that elusive job in PR.

Also, remember a tattoo is permanent – think before you ink:

Avoid the tattoo parlour while drunk;

Beware of oriental lettering;

Be sure of what it says;

And, no matter how much they beg or profess to have the skills, NEVER let your mate "do" you with their paint set and a knitting needle. In their uncle's basement.

UMBRELLAS

Whereas most people will tell you that they wouldn't be seen dead walking "out on road" in the rain, the rest of us who don't drive about town make do with umbrellas, coats, hoodies and hats to protect us from the elements.

There's also a Brolly Hierarchy to be aware of: this time it's the owner of the trendy golf or fishing brolly with the largest wingspan who gets the cheese. Those tiny ladies' handbag-sized pocket brollies suit tiny ladies (think of a frozen ready-prepared meal-for-one – as soon as it has to be shared with two or more people, you're in trouble).

One important thing to remember: even if you've got the right brolly and the rainfall to show it off, one powerful gust of wind is all it takes to propel it out of your hands and off to another country without you.

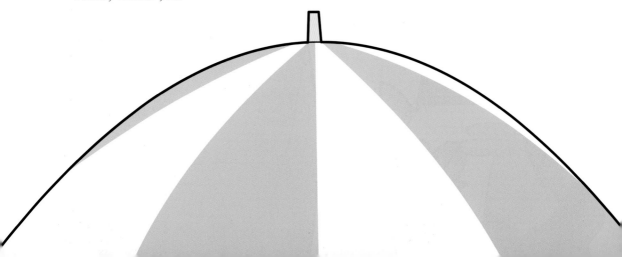

BABIES

What? BABIES?! What have they got to do with urban fashion? Listen, it's no joke: you sit at the bus stop reading your Sunday supplement and it's all celebs posing with babies on their arms, toddlers on shoulders. You look around you: school-age girls dressed up to the nines, posing with similarly dressed youngsters, little boxfresh trainers on tiny feet.

JUSEY, I NEED HELP. AM I CURSED WITH A LIFETIME OF BOUTIQUE-DISTRESSED DESIGNER DENIM?

NO! TRY MY..

NEW DIY DENIM DISTRESS KIT!

NOW WITH ADDED GOLDIDIUM!™

SET INCLUDES:

MA-HONEY.

HUNDREDS & THOUSANDS.

GOLD SPRAY PAINT.

..BUT WATCH OUT FOR BEES.

DANGER DANGER..

denim

Various versions:

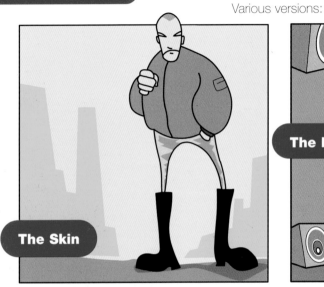

The Skin

The Roadie

The Woodstock

The Sag

camo

If you find yourself walking through town and you spy a large group of squaddies congregating in the doorway of a record shop, they're probably not squaddies at all but hardcore hip-hop heads, squabbling about which DJ's got the phattest beats in rap right now, or who's lyrically not doing it any more and should hang up the mic for good.

Whilst wearing this look, you attract disapproving frowns from the elderly. Remember, many of these people fought for their country and lost many friends and loved ones in the process. So the sight of mouthy youngsters seemingly misrepresenting their "colours" is bound to provoke some reaction or another.

Let it go.

wearing white

This aggressive but pristine-looking chap rushes to get on the Tube as the doors are closing. One impressive display of superhuman strength later, the doors are torn open and he's inside the carriage, defiantly smiling to himself. "What's so funny? Why are people smirking?"

It might look cool but you have to remember that everywhere is dirty. The slightest rub against most outdoor surfaces will leave an unsightly mark. No matter how faint or small, your whole day will be ruined because of it.

As for buying that fruity red drink, mmm, tastes good doesn't it? But can you really enjoy it with your poppy "minty-fresh" fashion? I think not, guv'nor.

wear your size

This is a slightly delicate area for some peeps, whether it applies to you personally or you feel it should be pointed out.

Firstly, we have to establish that we're referring to general urban wear as opposed to clubwear, because it's a whole different kettle of fish on the dancefloor. A basic rule of thumb is: if it looks or feels too tight, don't wear it.

Any form of physical activity – whether it be walking, shopping, working – you don't want your friends or colleagues to be whispering the words, "frayed thread" to you (or anyone else for that matter).

But when it comes to "big-boned women", I recommend treading extra carefully. She's proud of herself. Staring may result in a vicious and unblockable attack.

But remember, the same applies when attempting the overly-baggy style, thinking it's just as easy to raid your dad's wardrobe and end up looking like your granddad.

When you're out shopping, imagine you've been cordially invited to a round of golf with your posh mate and his dad, and you don't want to let the side down, so you have to look the part.

Diamond jumpers, pastel-coloured shirts, dogtooth-patterned three-quarter-length trousers tucked into the Argyll socks, bulbous golf shoes (complete with spikes) and a jauntily-angled flat cap to complete the look.

All this said and done, if the fit's not quite right, it's not going to work. Being aware of shop staff who have to make a certain number of sales that day, and will tell you that your oufit's "impeccable, sir", will save you a stack of money. Trust me.

chapter 3
entertainment

"When I first started going raving to the genre now known as UKG, it was all about the designer garms. I was living at home and worked in a pub for £3.50 an hour. I had no idea of the value of money. I once saved up for two months so I could go down Selfridges and buy some bright orange Moschino trousers and oversized black Versace shades. I drove to the rave in a clapped out, rust-ridden motor, with no more than tenner in my luminous back pocket, but it didn't matter, 'coz I was too busy looking gooood! All tags left on of course. Scary shit."

Elle J Small (urban music journalist/presenter)

Music, clubbing, dancing, drinking, drugs. None of that take your fancy? Brilliant, you'll be just fine and dandy then. What now? You've considered the museums, the galleries, the theatre, the circus, the library, the pub, playing board games in the hotel lobby. Surely there's more to it than this? Come now, you got cash and time on your hands – DO SOMETHING.

music
WHAT IS COOL?

You've just got off your plane/coach/whatever, dropped your suitcase to rush to the toilets, come out relieved and feeling about ten pounds lighter. You've gone to the nearest music outlet to update your still-pondwater-like CD collection, credit card at the ready… erm… Help?

It's so easy to be overwhelmed by the sheer enormity of what's on offer. As far as Urban goes, the sounds of now are definitely Rap, R&B, or UK Garage (which is refreshingly homegrown, so you don't have to get confused with imports and such); all of which are today's Pop – yesterday's Underground. The majority of today's chart acts have leaned heavily on these musical stylings to give them that much-desired street cred.

Back in the old days, these genres would have been hidden away in dingy record shop basements, with extortionate price tags and Temple of Doomesque stories of rare and exclusive trophies, never to be found anywhere else, or any cheaper.

Advertisement

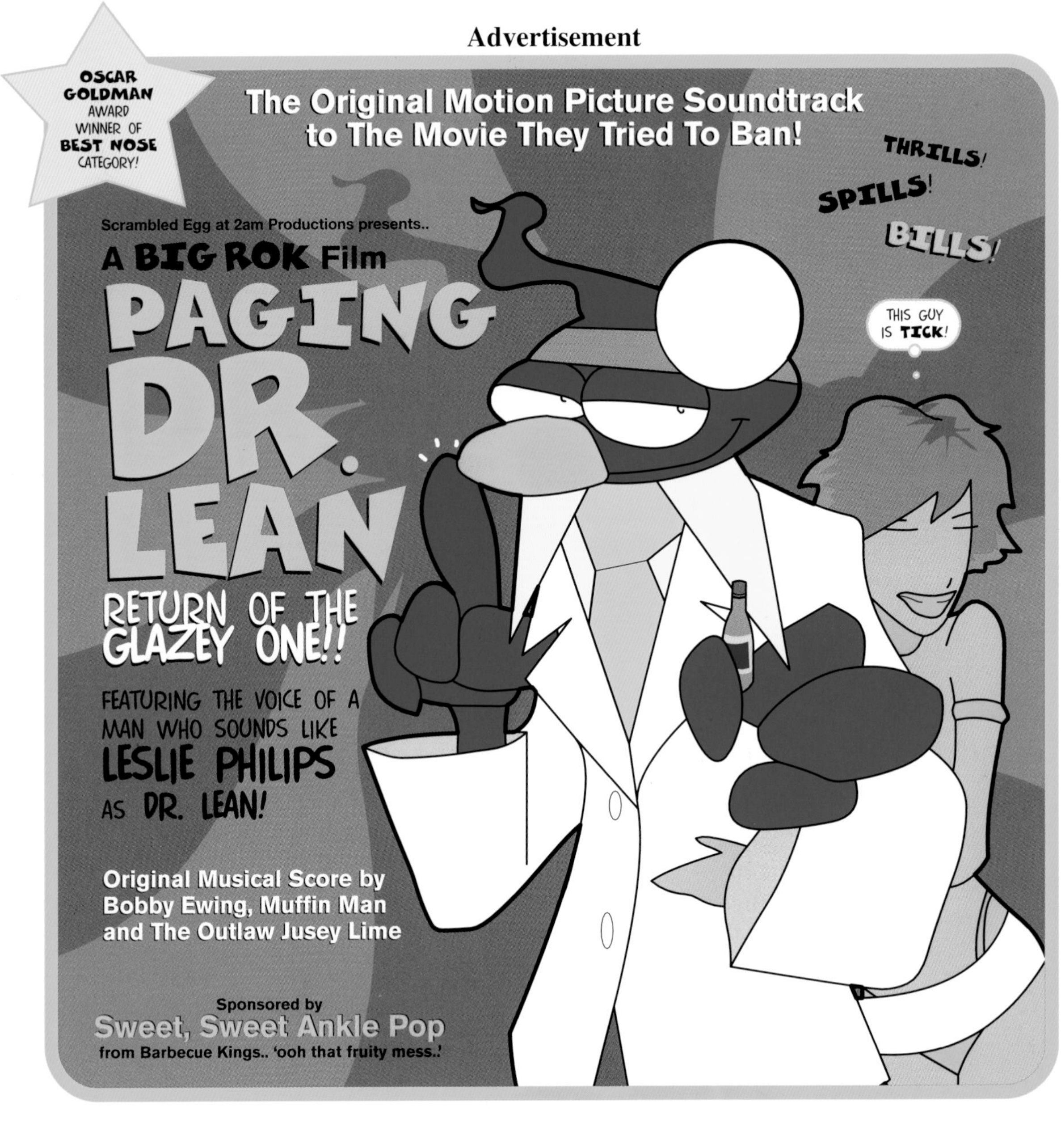

WHAT YOU KNOW ABOUT

You can't just turn around and say something as frivolous as, "Yeah, I know jazz", without incurring the wrath of the nearest die-hard jazz collector. Loosely spouting phrases like "Miles Coltrane is great" or "Thelonius Monkey's the bee's knees" will earn you a serious earache and possibly even a bloody nose. The safest bet is to assume that someone will always know more than you do.

YOU **WHAT**?!! YOU **PUNK**..

The only group of people more suspicious of amateur enthusiasts than jazz-hoarding trainspotters are Drum & Bass bods. You have Jungle, D&B, Hardcore, Darkcore, Progressive, Logical, blah blah, blee blee, and you cross these boundaries at your peril.

Simple parameters: Know What You Like, and Like What You Know. There's nothing really wrong with liking a bit of this and a bit of that, but if it's not truly your bag, and you overcompensate by learning the birthplace of your "idols", and what they ate around their nan's on a Friday afternoon, you'll end up becoming an Anorak. Knowing too much is almost as bad as knowing bugger all. Be Safe – Be Silent.

"We used to say that record shops had special speakers. We used to bowl into Groove Records in Greek Street and check out the latest tunes. They'd all sound amazing. I'd buy as many as I could with my weekend supermarket wages, then get home and play them and be like 'Is this the same tune? Must be the speakers!'

The best smell in the world was a fresh, sealed import 12-inch. They had to be sealed. Tried to open one like the guy in the shop, across the leg on his jeans – f*cked up my jumbo cords, man! I was never gonna get on *Dance Energy* with busted garms, man!"

DJ Swerve, KISS FM

CDs V VINYL

You may have noticed that many current club DJs use CDs and CD mixers as opposed to traditional records and turntables.

From a practical point of view, the advantages of CDs are endless: digital sound quality, seamless live mixing, PC CD-ROM compatibility, home CD burning, playing loud, crisp beats on your hi-tech in-car multi-stack CD changer (ICE = In Car Entertainment). And pushing your way through a packed club crowd with your CD selection in a snazzy purse instead of a standard record box (where a two-hour vinyl set can weigh as much as a hairy dwarf) can save time as well as your (and everyone else's) shins.

The advantages of vinyl?

Owning an original James Brown "Black Caesar" in an almost-impenetrable clear plastic sleeve; the static, crackles and all.

Universal Respect. Full Stop.

Genres: What do these terms mean?

"My first introduction to Jungle was in Essex, where ponytailed ravers dressed for bopping in the fields, off their faces on Rhubarb and Custards.

Meanwhile, in London, I found the dress code of clashing Versace jeans with Moschino shirts an offence to style.

I wanted to design for the ravers. So the Junglist Movement T-shirt was born. For me, the design summed up the whole scene: the two decks logo with the little acid house smiley face – the evolution of an underground movement."

Leke @ Aerosoul Ltd: Redefined Urban Threadz

www.aerosoul.com

The
Parallels of
Ballroom and
Bashment Dancing

clubs
PERSONAL HYGIENE

All I can say is: Guys – First Impressions Count.

There will always be those individuals who insist on stepping out without checking their "musk" level beforehand – doesn't matter if the clothes are clean, if you're putting them back on a dirty body, you might as well not bother. As for those "crufs" who will wear the same outfit day after day – brand-name sweater over shirt, over T-shirt, over string vest, over clammy body that's worked in a warehouse and on the shopfloor all afternoon, in summer – seems like they had put the evening garms under the work overalls from that morning ("Well, if there's no time to go home and change then at least I'm covered"). Punk – that's Nasty. Your mum would beat that carelessness out of you if she knew, and you know this.

Wash your hair. Wipe the sleep from your eye, and the white squall from the corner of your mouth. Shave your face, trim your beard and nasal hair. Check your "grill" for remnants of food ("Take that pork outta your smile"); use a moisturizer (I know loads of guys who would never admit to owning it, some who would never think of buying it; I say, "Who wants to look 40 when they're only 21?").

Check your nails are clean and trimmed, your "pits, nooks and crannies" have been dealt with prior to using talc, deodorant and aftershave. Brush those teeth, gargle with a reputable mouthwash (the Pound Shop brand doesn't have any real kick) and make sure you have a Pirate's stash of minty gum. All this should be an automatic response to the imminent prospect of being in close proximity to the opposite sex (you'd think so, wouldn't you?), but many a man still doesn't know the term:

"Check Yourself."

CHECKLIST

1. HAIR (WASH/COMB/STYLE)
2. FACE (WASH/SHAVE)
3. TEETH (BRUSH/FLOSS/GARGLE)
4. B.O (WASH/ANTIPERSPIRANT)
5. HANDS (WASH/NAILS/CREAM)
6. DOWNSTAIRS (WASH/TALC)
7. FEET/SOCKS (OBVIOUS)
8. TOOTHBRUSH & RAG
   (IN CASE YOU GO BACK TO HERS)
9. PROTECTION (CONDOMS)
10. MANNERS (OF COURSE)
11. LYRICS (AND AGAIN)
12. PEN & PAPER
    (HOW MANY TIMES HAVE YOU COME
    UNSTUCK WITHOUT THEM?)

GOOD LUCK MEN!

CHECK YOUR VENUES

"When I was 14, we all used to go out raving wearing all kinds of sh*t: white masks, white gloves, luminous orange London Underground coats, whatever. People loved it! One night we went to Jungle Soundclash at the Roller Express in Edmonton. Everyone gave us funny looks. These girls surrounded me and said, "You look like a right f*cking mug" and kicked me in the nuts! That was when I realized Hardcore and Jungle had become different types of music. Next time I went, I just wore a Hackett shirt!"

Matt Mason
Editor, *RWD Magazine*

CLUB

Yep, each night will entertain a completely different crowd, e.g. R&B night followed by S&M night. See how easy it is to confuse the two?

With the sheer volume of Information Access Points around us (Teletext, radio, text messaging, Internet, newspaper listings), for you to pretend that none of it exists and still go to the Line Dancing Night without your Cowboy Boots & Ten-Gallon Hat is just plain silly. Or, you might be trying a "double-bluff scam" – we already know how much you love rubber spikes and heels, chains and whips, squeaky toys and olive oil…

"It's simple, if we don't want someone to come in the club, they don't enter: 'Management Refuses The Right of Admission.' What can they say? If they want to kick up a fuss after that I'll say: 'Sorry, your mannerism does not suit this establishment.' "

Jay, Doorman

DOORMEN

You can never know where you stand when it comes to doormen. If you happen to know any of them personally, that alone is like having a "Get Out of Jail Free" card for your mates. As far as anyone knows, you could be the new owner of the club and you've just popped by to see how your Opening Night is progressing. If the doorstaff don't believe you, that Ring of Steel will Not Be Breached. (Forget it. Sack 'em in the morning.)

If your checklist for the night included sweets, tissues, mints, gum, etc., then be prepared to give it up like Harvest Festival. There's a bucket at the entrance where all that goodness is going – mark my words. If you still want that personal freedom unrestricted, Stash Your Stuff. Doesn't matter where: in your sock, in your underwear, in your partner's underwear, behind your belt buckle, in the lining of your Trilby – wherever.

A general tip: incitement to violence is on a hair trigger, so avoid making conversation (unless you are prompted). If you're feeling particularly tenacious, take a record box, wear a baseball cap low over your eyes and picture yourself at the bar, smugly sipping alcoholic freebies through a curly straw. Well, it might work…

"When blagging to get into a club, always appear calm, as if you're not the one making a mistake about you not being on the guestlist. It's just a matter of time before they let you in!"

Ty

Keep your eyes on the prize. Be co-operative if there seems to be any turbulence during your transition from outside to inside. Sometimes the only obstacle between you and the Holy Grail is the Guestlist Girl. She has the power to make or break your night. She doesn't care. It makes her feel good. So it's out of your hands. Think positive thoughts.

THE CLOAKROOM

You finally make it through the main doors, but the tension hasn't subsided yet. Now you're thinking, "If it's a quid per item, how many items can I roll up and stuff into the sleeves, only paying for one?" A lot of nightclubs have a 'Compulsory Cloakroom' – meaning, "You **will** take your jacket off."

Because if you don't, somebody else definitely will (without paying attention to the intricate stitching or lining).

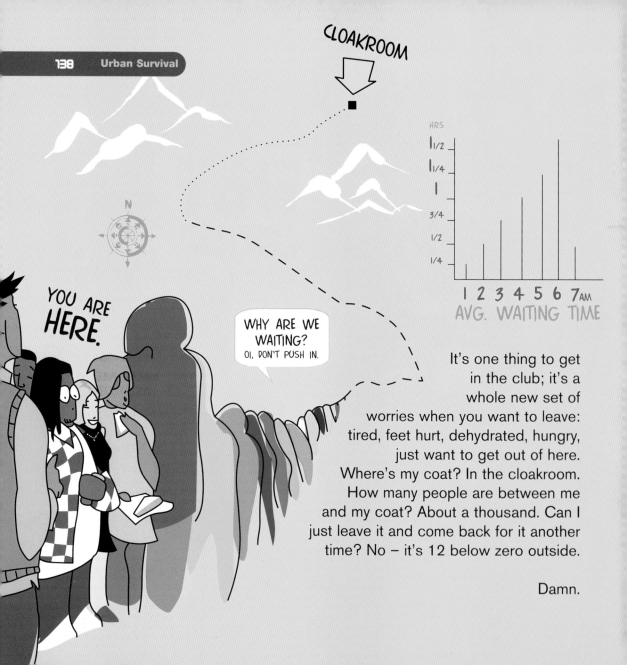

NO, I DON'T BELIEVE IT. I'VE LOST MY TICKET.

AHHHAARRRGGH...!!

Actually: before you even start queueing, where's your ticket? "Erm… erm… I put it in this pocket… No, this one. No… didn't I give you my ticket to hold? What you saying? **Bitch, gimme my ticket!!"**

It's no wonder you'll see dozens of young women with next-to-nothing on, walking briskly along the high street, properly goosebumped-up.

Guys: remember it's rude to stare, and be a gent – offer the poor girl your coat.

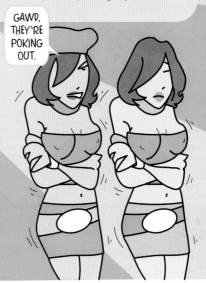

GAWD, THEY'RE POKING OUT.

"You know what pisses me off as a DJ when I go to a club to play? Nine times out of ten the equipment is faulty, the turntables are a mile apart, there's nowhere to put your records – and I Still Manage TO ROCK THE PARTY!!!!!"

DJ 279, Choice FM

SORRY LOVE, I AIN'T DOING NO REQUESTS.

BUT IT'S MY BIRTHDAY PARTY.

TOUGH.

DJs & MCs

These characters are the key to your night out going with a Bang or a Little Farty Whimper. As a result, their egos can be a little hard to contain at times. If they are anywhere near as Big as they say they are, technically your punters should get their money's worth.

What you also may notice is the heated competition between DJs from different sets, crews or radio stations: individuals who purposefully play over their designated time slot can even wind up the coolest of cats.

"When I first started DJing, I found I had to be confident and sometimes even aggressive towards certain male DJs (mostly unknowns with something to prove). On a few occasions, the DJ before me would try and play overtime and into my set. I say 'try' 'cos there was NO WAY I was taking that sh*t just because I'm female! That mentality has stayed with me, and backfired the other day when I bullied a DJ off the decks, determined to play my set. After 40 minutes I realized I was in the wrong club!!"

Emma Feline

Whatever you do, don't mention the words "Open Mic", unless you know exactly what it means: having your Ice Cream and Jelly Party (complete with innocent young nieces and nephews) distressed and turned upside down by crews of rival MCs looking to settle their "beef" inside your Function Room. And all that foul language is making you edgy – "Can somebody **please** disconnect the power?"

"One time, in a club in Manchester, an MC asked me if he could spit on the mic. It wasn't my mic, so I said yes. Not five minutes later a next MC came. Within 15 minutes the DJ box was full of MCs spitting on the mic! One of them turned to me and said, 'Can't you come out the DJ box? Because I can't move!' I wanted to come out anyway as all that spit was making the floor slippy!"

Oris Jay

WORLD'S GREATEST DANCER?

Yep, those people who feel the need to take up the most space, doing the urban equivalent of the Square Dance – the ritual marking of the "ring". You're never quite sure of the boundaries. Is it that every point on the dancefloor they've stepped into counts as "their" land? Are you allowed to step there? How long do you leave it vacant, without fear of the "owner" returning? Certain guys will actually indicate to other males that they are only going to the loo, and will be back soon, so "don't even think about it". This he communicates with a few strategic facial expressions.

Some have a habit of sprinkling champagne on the floor, creating a "perimeter", reminiscent of animals in the wild marking their territory with their scent. Is it to attract females for mating purposes? Is it designed to let other pretenders and haters know that there can only be One Alpha Male; One King?

A possible method of restoring the balance of power is to ask your largest mate (nicely) to act as a bulldozer, edge backwards into the disputed area and take back the land – "Sorry, I never saw you there, bruv."

"UNCLE"?

You know the guy: he's upped the average age of the crowd a little bit; and, no, he's not really old – just too old to be in *that* club. If it was an over-40s Soca dance, or even a "Blues" in someone's house, it wouldn't look so bad.

If the guy was out on the town with the wife, spending a few hours over a lovely meal and it was too early to go home, so they treated themselves to a little "buck-and-weave" on the nearest dancefloor showing the youngsters how it should be done, that shouldn't be frowned on either. (Yes, there would be some sniggering at the back – "Glad that's not my mum and dad", etc. – but so what? They're not bothered, so why should you be?)

No, it's when he's running up on girls too young for his daughter to play with, telling them "Who's the daddy?" whilst rubbing his musk-saturated chest wig on their torso, heavy gold ingot waving around recklessly in the vast chasm of his shirt's opening…

"When it comes to men, play it cool. Never chase a man ... let him chase you."

Alesha, Mis-teeq

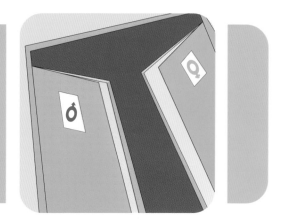

Look around. Everyone is scoping everyone else out, on the hunt for "some action". Large groups of guys posing and posturing; little gaggles of females, blatantly aware of the number of hungry males who are peeping, patiently waiting for any signal that tells them their advances have been assessed and are finally welcome.

Just like in the wild, it takes a brave few to branch away from the pack and set up their pitch directly at the entrance to the WC, vastly increasing their odds of getting "first dibs" on the available ladies. This takes nerves of steel though, because being this close puts you in the line of fire for a public "Blast": the ultimate in humiliation. If everyone (including the other males) sees you getting the "Talk-to-the-Hand" gesture, your chances of success with anyone else that night are reduced to nothing – no scoop for you. Then your rivals are free to pick up where you left off, knowing you are officially out of the picture.

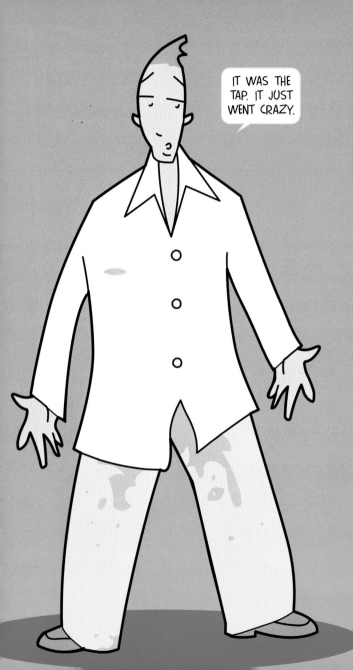

Guys – beware of "splashback". Do the maths:

(Urinals + light-coloured trousers = ?)

You came out tonight with the intention of going home with "something saucy"? Might as well get your coat now, bruv, 'cos you ain't pulling. You can mouth the words, "It's not what you think, it's beer" all you want over the loud music – it's too late. The damage is done.

Your credit has run out.
Step away from the bar.

SMOKING

To the uninitiated, having a box of cigarettes seems like having a few good mates with you: you'll never be alone. In even the most hostile or boring of environments you can maintain that air of confidence, mystery and intrigue just by seductively lighting one up.

If you do smoke, and you've bought enough supplies to last you the night, our advice is to keep it to yourself (unless you want to be the handy dancefloor vendor for the rest of the night). Overfriendly strangers will lurk at your perimeter, hoping to catch your eye (which acts as the catalyst for a hopelessly banal conversation, and always ends in "…ain't got a spare snout, have you mate?")

GOT A SPARE FAG, BIG BOY?

Please Note: Smokers smell smoky. If you were intending to "get your smooch on" that night, bear in mind that you can't have it both ways: either you can't stand the way they taste or they can't stand the way you smell. When in the all-night grocer, there's always the person who says something obscure like, "Don't worry about getting me any food. As long as I got me fags, I'll be sweet."

No you won't. You'll be starving.

WOMEN WHO STING YOU FOR DRINKS

"Hi there. Sorry to bother you, but it's my mate's birthday today. Would you mind buying her a drink?"

Does this type of banter ring a bell? I'm sure it will bring back painful and expensive memories for some of you. For those of you who haven't been stung yet, be on your guard.

What's wrong with buying a drink for a woman? Nothing at all; it's the deceitful way she went about it. Of course you'll feel nice for a moment because, judging by the eyes you were getting, there's a distinct possibility that this could be your night, squire. The friend drapes herself around your neck like a feather boa, and whispers very suggestively into your ear (words like "ménage", and such), which ups the ante considerably. If you thought you could ignore the bait before, you're definitely hooked now.

So you buy them a round. Then, with tie loosened, you await their return from the "Ladies' Room". Half an hour later, pulse returned to normal, bored, you wander round the club, curiosity having got the better of you. To your horror, you come across the girls "nicing up" a couple of smilers, convinced they've just scored.

Hold on a minute – wasn't it the other girl's birthday?

> **"When clubbing, make sure you wear comfortable clothes, especially shoes ... go for flat soles every time – there's no point breaking your foot for fashion"**
>
> Su Elise, Mis-teeq

SENSIBLE SHOES?

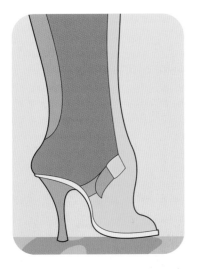

Does that girl over there look comfortable in those heels? It probably went something like this: She saw The Shoes – she's gotta buy them. Can she walk in them? Doesn't matter. Will they have her size? Doesn't matter. Will they impress the guys? 'Course they will. That's all that matters, isn't it?

Club night. Time to christen the shoes. Toenails painted, ankle chain on. Er – how is a girl supposed to walk in these 6-inch heels if they're too small (2 sizes to be exact)? Let's assume she got a cab, because there's no way she got on any bus and walked anywhere in those.

Don't know how she's going to get up or downstairs, how she's going to dance, go to the toilet or make it over to the bar to get her drink. You'll know her when you see her, because she'll be the one who hasn't moved from the same spot since she got there; she's dancing with her mid-section; and her friend is getting the drinks for both of them. Before you even look at her and think, "Hey, she looks nice. Kinda mysterious," don't even bother. Watch her for a bit. Think to yourself, "Are her feet hurting?"

 the doc says:

Guys – watch your target. If you see her regularly touching or even looking at her own toes or heel whilst grimacing, that's a fair indication that there will be no "quick-quick-slow" with that particular young lady tonight. Try again next week.

WHY THE HELL AM I DOING THIS?

CAN I HAVE THIS DANCE?

NO.

ALCOPOPS

Snazzy, jazzy, zingy, new-wave, original ways of experimenting with alcohol or just old fogey drinks revamped with berries and fizz? Of course, making whisky taste like cherryade is obviously going to result in a generation of pre-teen alcoholics. What next:

"Rum Gumballs"?

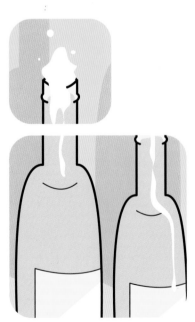

DANCES ARE NOT INTERCHANGEABLE...

...between clubs, i.e. "big-box-little-box" will not work in a bashment dance; nor will a "slow crub" be welcomed at a Drum & Bass rave.

THE HARBOUR SHARK

Aka the **3am Desperado**; these daring opportunists know the club's only Three Slow Numbers away from closing. Regular as clockwork, the DJ's cued up the Smoochy Set; most punters have made their way to the cloakroom, apart from a few couples and a (very) few single females.

It's almost as if they're just waiting to be ravaged.

Unless you are a seasoned regular, all the various dancefloor customs can appear quite confusing to the untrained spectator's eye. So if it does in fact get too much for you, at least you can rest in the knowledge that you can "sit this one out": find an unoccupied spot by the wall (a nigh-impossible feat in itself), put your hood up and lean back, folding your arms.

And while you're there, you might as well check your voicemail messages.

CLUBBING HOLIDAYS

Ayia Napa, Ibiza… you know the deal. Sun, sea, sand (sex, scoring, stories, STDs, stupidity, sick everywhere, shame, stink, seen-on-TV, "sloppy seconds", spitting, shouting, smashed-in-the-face, sunglasses, swelling, shopping, sipping Sangria, sleeping, sunburnt, stinging, shuffling back to hotel, swearing):

"I'M NEVER COMING BACK HERE AGAIN!! **NEVER!!!**"

Until next season – start saving. It's how you spend your hard-earned wages, what you wait all year for. So if you're not up for meeting the gang out there, last two weeks in July, because you're staying in a caravan down the coast with your family, keep it to yourself – nobody wants to know.

TAKEAWAY ON THE WAY HOME – THE DANGERS

You've just spilled out of the nightclub and the effect of the alcohol you've consumed that night is starting to wear off, leaving you Absolutely STAR-AR-VING.

Bleary-eyed, you glance round towards the Light – the Light of the neon Doner Kebab sign. Your nose moves first, pulling your head forward, then the rest of your body follows – staggering and salivating like a zombie. You haphazardly negotiate the other clubbers sitting on the kerb, clutching their kebab wrappers, polystyrene boxes, containing centre-of-the-earth-hot chips and salad (mainly red cabbage and whole chillies – you'd think that if they didn't want them, they would have told the guy "no salad" when he asked, instead of screwing up their faces and dumping handfuls of mess in the road or on the shop floor, right in front of the fruit machine), or unsafely stacked quarter pounders (squeeze the bun in the wrong place and you can kiss goodbye to that four quid; the contents of that burger would be on the floor).

A half-hour wait to be served (by which time you've witnessed countless lives being threatened, women screaming, relationships ending, others beginning, endless graphic tales of sexual conquest – funnily enough, none of failure and missed opportunity; if you scored tonight, guys, what are you doing in here?), then your turn comes.

"Can I help you, my friend?"

On the whole this is a dodgy option: you're better off scooting off home as quick as you can, then filling the biggest Pyrex dish with Swiss Style Muesli and a pint of milk. Do you really want the onion breath in the morning (even after brushing)? Or the extremely bad tummy upset? Fatty chicken, covered in hair, grease oozing, unidentified lumps of semi-opaque gristle?

drugs

Come on, son, **What You After?** We got Rocks, we got Bones, we got Brown, we got Stones. Got the Skunk, got the Punk, we got the Sess, it's Blessed. If you're broke, it's Commerc(ial) you smoke. Oh Please, of course I got Es, I've even got Acid, Hardcore Amphetamines. Got the Downers, got Uppers, got Ketamine for the nutters (oh, that'll make you flatline). They're all sublime, anytime at the Friendly Neighbourhood Frontline.

Last year it was calculated that there were approximately 15,000 robberies in one known 'Crack Spot' which doubles as the latest Trendy Hangout for Urbanites"; bored with the usual West End haunts and want to be seen "Walking on The (borderline of) Wild Side"… for The Scourge. The Devil. The Beginning And The End. It's Where All The Money Goes and Why Sh*t Happens.

But still they seem to be an integral part of culture, whether you're For or Against. Many have tried something just once, and for them, life has never been the same since.

So I guess the main advice would be that old cliché: **"If you can't be good, be safe."** Learn about what's out there, use a bit of common sense and trust your instincts: don't let anyone force you into anything.

You might think you would recognize a dealer if you saw one, no problem. Well, good luck mate. Trust me, these days it's all about business. Think about it: if someone's trying to make sales, the less conspicuous they look, the more chance they'd have at a regular custom without fear of detection.

Now you can't be seen as just any geek off the street, even if you are. These vultures wouldn't bat an eyelid after selling you a foil wrap of dried pigeon poop and swearing blind that "This is the stuff that will make your nature rise". HA! You're better off going around with a little spoon yourself and getting it straight from the… horse's, er, mouth… so to speak.

I'm sure I don't have to hold your hand in every single situation, but there must come a time when I shouldn't have to tell you:

"Don't Mug Yourself."

REALLY, IF YOU SKIPPED THE "GETTING HAMMERED" PART OF YOUR WEEK, TOOK THAT MONEY AND BUILT YOURSELF A RECORDING STUDIO IN THE BASEMENT, GOT YOUR FAT TUNE PUT ON A DUB PLATE, ETC.

SOMETHING'S ON WOODY'S MIND.

CHEMIST

I CAN'T SEE WHY THAT SO-CALLED "CHEMIST" IN THE CLUB HAD TO GIVE ME THE RUNAROUND. I MIGHT AS WELL GO DOWN TO THE ONE IN THE HIGH STREET TO GET MY "SCORE".

NOW THE CHAP SAID I SHOULD GET ME SOME ASH, BANGERS & MASH, CRASHBANGWALLOPS, DOO-DOOS, EGGS'N'BACON, FLIP-FLOPS, GOOD STUFF, HARD BOILEDS, INK, JUNGLE JUICE, KOSHER...

PRESCRIPTIONS

...LIQUORICE, MUSTARD, NAPALM, OXO CUBES, POPPERS, QUIDDICH, RASTA-FOUREYES, SHROOMS, TOOTIES, UM BONGOS, VA-VA-VOOMS, WILLY WONKAS, X-RAYS, YATTIES AND ZOOTIES.

PRESCRIPTIONS

YOU GET THE HELL OUT OF MY ESTABLISHMENT, BEFORE I GET IGNORANT.

I'M SORRY, YOU MEAN YOU DON'T STOCK ANY OF THE AFOREMENTIONED ITEMS?

You might vaguely recall the satisfactory image of yourself in the mirror many moons ago. Understand, this doesn't apply any more: completely sweated through to the skin, the combined aromas of "Dr Funk eau de toilette", ciggy smoke, alcohol breath and some other smell "a bit like burning polystyrene" do not make for a pleasant bouquet or an irresistable pheromone for the opposite sex.

> **"You know Certain Bouncers are making a wedge on the side by running scams with the dealers; let them in on the guestlist so they can do business; split the profits afterwards."**
>
> Clayton, TOV Music

What goes up must come down. If you take off hard, you'll come down hard, simple maths. You had a banging night, you loved everyone. You kissed loads of people (were they male or female? Can't remember, who cares?) If you had anything important to do the next day, forget it – it's not going to happen.

If you were lucky, you steered clear of all that excitement, and settled with a few trial-sized bottles of Low Alcohol French Ale. You had a little knee-shake in the corner, didn't go too wild, got your bottom groped by a mature lady with a big smile and "Follow-Me-Back-To-New-Cross-Eyes", which you politely declined. You just had a quick dash to the loo before the long journey home. Standing in the cubicle, you heard a whisper behind you:

"Sorry mate, weren't you finished? Couldn't do us a favour, could ya?"

funfairs

GHOST TRAIN

Dodgen

Bumper cars: the only cool attraction to hang out by. The Waltzer: makes you incredibly dizzy, even sick, but it's cool to go on in order to impress. You just need to "style it out" afterwards. And make yourself scarce.

ARCADES

Most guys will never properly shrug off the addictive, sticky allure of the amusement arcade. Women will swoon at your manliness.

And if you look closely, you'll notice that no one really eats candy floss any more – just like kebabs, they taste exactly the same as you remember them, it's just that you're on your own now.

"You don't really wanna buy that, do ya?

That's not even real food.
Behave yourself!"

HAVE YOU ANY
IDEA OF HOW
RIDICULOUS
THAT LOOKS?

chapter 4
getting around

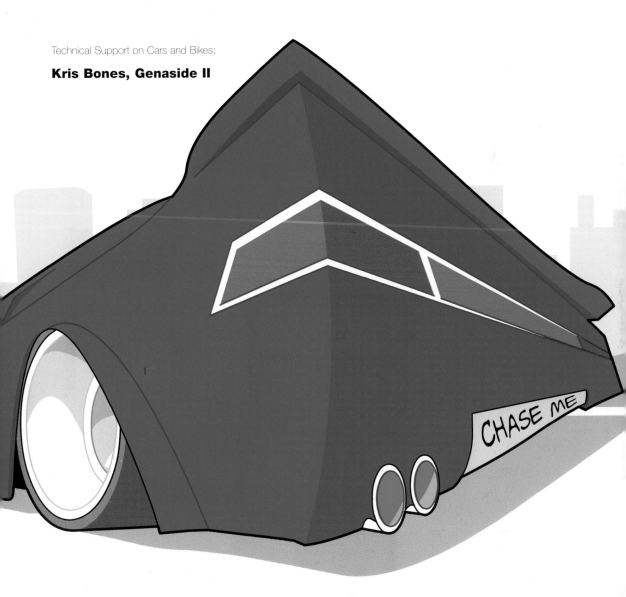

Technical Support on Cars and Bikes:

Kris Bones, Genaside II

public transport

As you stand there in the freezing rain, sighing, "At Last! The Bus is Actually Coming… wait a minute… is he actually gonna stop?" What you must realize is that these hard-working members of the community get NO RESPECT WHATSOEVER. Therefore, you have to make yourself stand out (literally) from the rest of society in general. Wear something fluorescent if you have to, because you screaming at the back of the bus after it's zoomed past the stop will get you absolutely NOWHERE!!

"Upstairs on my school bus was for **Second Years** and upwards. You had to earn that seat up there. It was that mythical Heaven where all the "good" people were – the ones that you wanted to be like and be liked by. The hardest guys were there, the fittest girls, the funniest jokers. So when I got there (in the First Year, actually) I had to go undercover: sit at the front, keep my eyes forward and never, **NEVER** look at anyone on the back seat as you went down the stairs!

The **Unwritten Rules** that everyone on the 194 bus knew. It was only when I worked my way through the school years and earned my Back Seat status around about the Fourth Year that I realized it was all bullsh*t and in my head. Being upstairs just meant you stank of smoke and had to convince your mum it wasn't you, as those were the days when it was legal to do that on a bus. The other main health hazard was negotiating the stairs as it went round that corner just before your stop!!"

Soliheen the Wisechild

It's late; you're tired; everyone's tired; even the driver's yawning (it's a wonder we didn't all end up in the Thames a minute ago). So what if the bus smells a bit? All you can think of is making yourself a nice Hot Choccie in a Big Mug, listening to Jazz FM with the volume barely audible, your scented bedside lamp, putting on your "fresh-off-the-bathroom-radiator" fluffy PJs (or even better, climbing into your natural-body-heated bed into your partner's warm patch). Yep – let me just fluff these pillows…

Wait a minute. Those aren't pillows!

"OI! WHAT YOU DOING?!! YOU LOOKING TO GET KNOCK OUT, STAR?!!"

You manage to find a little corner seat (downstairs);
you fall asleep; you wake up somewhere in Kent.

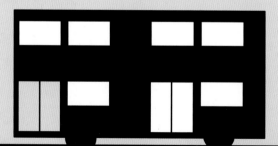

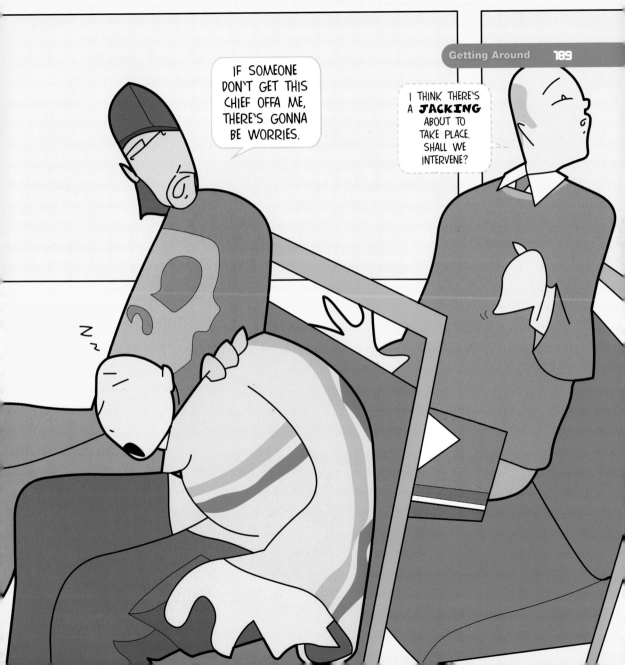

ON THE TUBE

"There are many reasons why I don't like getting the Tube. Here are just a few:

1. When you change lines, the trek is SO long that you might as well have walked in the first place (maybe they could introduce mini-Tubes to ferry us between platforms).
2. Being short means I have to push harder to get on the Tube first for those much-prized doorway/ glass partition cool leaning positions.
3. Never touch your face with your hands after you've been on the Tube until you've washed them with some industrial-strength antibacterial hand soap. All those sweaty 'early morning – couldn't be bothered to wash' mitts mixed with 'end of the day – been to the loo at work but haven't washed my hands once despite seeing the Health-&-Safety poster in the office toilet' paws. Rub your eyes at your peril!!

And finally –

4. **'Tube Nose': Go on, give it a good blow after a day's Underground hopping... I don't know what it is but it's black and hard and that can't be good!"**

Mary Joy, Singer

You've had a nightmare of a day: you're having a hard time breaking in those shoes; you've been running your heart out; you finally get to the carriage doors and a cheeky sort in a suit puts his hand up like he's stopping traffic.

"Sorry, love. No room in this one."

Three 'Shoulder Drops' and a 'Figure-Four Leg Lock' later, you're on the train.. only to find a surly young chap with his feet up on the seat opposite.

"Excuse me, can I sit down, please?"

He stares at you, emotionless. You can hardly contain your anger.

"Would you let your own mother stand while you spread out all over the place?"

"It's always the same with them and us: 'You think you own the road!'... 'At least I got a licence!'-type of thing. We all do the same job, mate."

Nobby, South London cabbie

TAXIS V MINICABS

If you've just been paid and you don't mind splashing out, flying around in a Black Cab has great advantages: your whole crew can fit in the back, and you don't have to worry about dodgy suspension slowing the car down – if you can actually get one to stop for you in the first place.

Minicabs are a much better mode of transport if you live outside the city centre (need to get the shopping home, or bring your portable TV & video to your mate's house for the night); they'll go Anywhere and pick up Everyone (as long as there's only a few of you – if you do happen to get four or more in the car, the back axle will be the first to get dropped off, forget making it all the way home).

They know how much the fare is, but don't know how to get there (beyond having a vague recollection of the bus route).

You step out of the club **sweating**. Now it's "Home, James." To step out of the mist without your head down, stepping hard towards your car, is to attract The Swarm of Killer Bees. Triple-parked, partially obscuring oncoming traffic, they don't care. A fare's a fare – however you get it.

Word of Warning: To minimize the odds of a bad cabbing experience, make sure there's nobody else inside the cab before you get in; make small talk but don't overdo it; determine the fare with the Controller (if there is one) before you set off; and if you are "on your Jones", always sit in the back.

A TYPICAL SCENARIO.

cars

"THE SOUND OFF" – CAR AUDIO COMPETITION

First things first: do not put your head in the car – any car. The dangers of permanent hearing damage are real. Also, requests are a no-no. If you're new to these events, eating a hearty meal just before the contest may result in violent projectile vomiting caused by extreme Sub Bass frequencies.

At the car show you'll hear a lot of completely alien terms like:

Engine transplant: Moving an engine from one car to another.

Trick bits: Polished after-market goodies.

Quarter-mile time: How fast your car goes up the dragstrip.

Also – cams, carbon this and that, 16V, port & polish, light and balanced, four-branch, venier pulley, bored out to, K&N, ECU, hybrid, DTM, camber, 4 pot, 4WD, 1.7 bar, 30psi...

OOH OOH. THEY'RE SOME PHAT RIMS.

"YA RIDE"

Bigger wheels (rims): For example, "rollin' on 20s" – better; shinier, chromier, "eat your dinner off 'em" – better; skinnier-profile tyres – better.

Suspension: Only one rule – decked. On the floor, scratching like the Batmobile, can't turn, wheels touching body – LOW!

Body: Wide arches, big bumpers, chin & boot spoilers, tinted windows.

Flipmode colours: ("GAWD! It changed colour as it passed!").

ICE (In Car Entertainment)**:** More speakers than Woodstock; subwoofers of insane sound depth; amps with more power than the National Grid; SPL (Sound Pressure Level) 170dB (twice as loud as Concorde); going as low as 15Hz (with human hearing starting at 17Hz).

Engine: NOS (Nitrous Oxide); turbocharger dump valve (for the "whooosh"); large CCs (cubic capacity), for that sick growl; largest exhaust, louder the better; BHP (Brake Horse Power), the more the better.

RAGGO 1

> **"Don't ever let a car rule you; walk as much, as often, until you've made your cash. Then buy whatever you want. Peace."**
>
> Dave Angel

Regardless of the time of day (usually very early morning, or late at night), you'll notice these drivers, stationary at the traffic lights or in a jam, with a post-"Blues" hangover; either on the mobile or having a conversation with their fellow passengers. The whole street needs to be shaking in time to the music (heavy Dub, Garage or Ragga) blasting from mighty speakers. He's sitting right underneath the windscreen, pulling odd "driving faces", going around harmless corners and roundabouts gurning and leaning in the direction of travel, bobsleigh-style. He says it helps with manoeuvrability.

I bet it does.

CARJACKING

After witnessing the obvious joy found by the guy in the arcade, living out his Crime Fantasy, maybe we should point out that driving games and real life are not to be confused. Today's gangster-themed films and games feature you as the Ultimate Getaway Driver and Carjacker..

'Who jacked the jacker,
who jacked the carjacker,
who thought he'd never get jacked?'

You've got to know how the land lies, have an idea of what's going on around you. If some madman is willing to stick a gun barrel in your ear or, even worse, threaten to kidnap your child, over a car?! Let it go people, it's not worth it, insurance will cover that. Go home to your family in one piece, they'll love you for it.

TAILGATING & ROAD RAGE

"What you sitting on my f**** bumper for?! That f****** idiot's been up my a*** for too long now – I'll show him."** This, followed by a short, sharp "mash" on the brakes – almost resulting in a nasty back-end collision (matter of inches). "That'll teach you!"

Is This You?

Don't even try and deny it. The basic pressures of city life – the Rat Race. Everyone needs to be Somewhere Else. Everyone also needs some sort of tension release. It could be a five-minute journey that takes an hour and a half. Life at home ain't too great either. All this stress build-up is extremely dangerous if left unchecked. Right about now, that person's percolating, ready to blow. Don't say anything like, "Cheer up, it may never happen," because it probably already has.

The thing about Road Rage is the name itself. As soon as they put a name to it, everyone jumped at the opportunity to find a logical, medical reason for getting out of your car, going to your boot for something heavy – "Hmm… I'll think I'll take the wheel brace. No, better still, I'll go for the carjack" – as an instructional device to convince the other driver that, although you might have a pleasant smile and good teeth, you are not above "wetting up a next man if push come to shove".

Problem is, how do you measure "reasonable force"? An altercation takes place, somebody gets hurt (quite severely), Old Bill shows up and forget trying to conceal or toss the offensive weapon down a grass verge – these days you'll find CCTV everywhere if you look hard enough. Someone saw you doing something, it's only a matter of time. Even if you didn't actually swing your makeshift "Excalibur", the mere fact that you were brandishing it in a threatening manner is enough to get you up on one charge or another.

"Duck down, Pompeii, 'cos I'm coming, ready or not," said Mt Vesuvius.

Be honest. Didn't matter who it was. Someone was going to get an earful from you today – whether it was the night security staff, the cleaner, the boss' dog, the parking attendant sitting in that "poxy little box", the girl at the other end of the drive-through fast-food restaurant speakerphone, that guy on crutches taking too long on the zebra crossing…

This birthday, tell your family you only want Classical Music CDs for the car.

HOLDING UP TRAFFIC

Picture it: you're in a desperate hurry to get across town, thinking to yourself, "Which route should I take? I know what I'll do – blaze down that road, cut across there, go through that gap, slip behind Such and Such, zoom down Whassisname, then, Bob's your uncle, I'm there!" Tyres squealing, your plan seems like it's going to work just fine: "…shouldn't be any traffic down here this time o' day… OH CRAP!!!! WHYYYYY???!!!"

Same ol' sh**, same old lane. Two guys acting like they haven't seen each other since nursery decide to have a mother's meeting right there in the middle of the road, totally oblivious to the number of vehicles backed up in both directions behind both of their brand-new sporty convertibles. It wouldn't be so bad if this wasn't part of a single-decker bus route (for people carrying heavy shopping, children and the elderly). Now you're bursting to say something in protest, along the lines of: **"Please could you move your car, so the rest of us can get past?"**

That one move could get you shot and killed. Is it worth it? Bus drivers find it easier to park up and call the police – passengers or no passengers. You know what your next sensible move is? Take out your mobile, call whoever it was you were meeting and postpone until tomorrow, turn off the engine, take off your shoes, cue up your Lover's Rock compilation CD on the stereo, push your seat back into a reclining position – and chill.

"RIDING SHOTGUN" V BACK SEAT

Right, you and your mates are about to go out in the car; doesn't matter where. You might notice there will always be one person, and always the SAME person, who will stop at nothing to ensure that they get the front passenger seat, no matter who they wind up to get their way. Usually a thick skin will protect them from being affected by everyone else's body language and retaliatory gestures. The driver doesn't really care who sits next to 'em, it's just annoying that the permanent seat cover suggests that being up front makes you more important than the "underlings" in the back. It's as if being seen in the front on a regular basis somehow entitles you to a share of the car. This obviously means that you can borrow the keys, any time you need to take someone you just met in the club somewhere private, to "get to know them better".

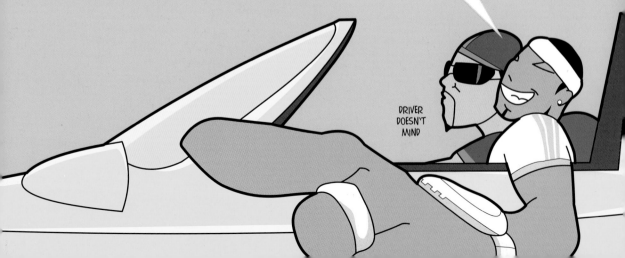

HEY BABY, WHERE YOU OFF TO? YOUR SURNAME MUST BE SPANNER 'COS YOU JUST MADE MY NUTS TIGHTEN.

DRIVER DOESN'T MIND

You get the feeling that this obsessive behaviour stems from bitter childhood memories of being made to feel like a caged animal by their parents, after being shouted at for hitting a younger sibling on a seven-hour drive back from a long, tiring day out at the coast. On a proper sulk.

Other factors that may contribute to this almost allergic reaction to the back seat could be: you always see criminals handcuffed and bundled into the back of police squad cars, then as they're driven away they either have that sorrowful or that vengeful look on their faces; seeing docile family pets cooped up under the back window of the station wagon, bored to tears due to the lack of space; or unruly children banished there until they get home.

DESIGNATED DRIVER

Many crews will have only one or two guys that can legally drive – one car between at least ten people. Everybody wants to go out but nobody wants to go out in the cold to "Bus It".

"Yo – it's Proper Parky out tonight, geez. Y'won't catch me out there at all, rudeboy… (long, silent pause)… unless you're up for picking me up from my girl's gaff about 11? Come on, mate. You know you have to pass mine to go uptown anyway. Well, alright, then, 15 minutes drive **past** your house, but you know how it is – if I had a car, you know I'd be driving us everywhere. What's that? When am I gonna pass my test? How many times you gonna bug me about that same thing? I told you, as soon as I got the funds to get my TT."

You'll get an unpopular guy looking for a "bring-in", who might hurry and get his wheels on the quiet, just so he can win friends & respect; or the entrepreneur of the crew, who doesn't mess about when it comes to asking for petrol cash.

"Oi! Empty your pockets, fools! I ain't paying for this on my Jacks!"

Getting a fiver off everyone would make him at least £50 for the night, and he wouldn't have to buy any rounds.

motorbikes

Making your way around the city by car is relatively straightfoward. It can be quite demanding mentally but you're more or less protected within the confines of your car. For some, the thought of having their timetable dictated to them by traffic congestion, roadworks, contraflow systems, diversions, etc. has led them to free themselves of the normality and safety of the car altogether, and take to just two wheels – two **fast** wheels – as their means of transport.

Just getting around is simply not enough for everybody, though. It's how you do it that matters. How you show what you've learnt, what you've done to your machine after countless hours in the garage.

Any opportunity for a quick race, burnout or over-the-tank wheelie is passionately grabbed:

Any Excuse.

A DAY IN THE LIFE OF A ... bike freak

Checking the Teletext hourly the night before for the weather report, Wifey asks if you could take her shopping tomorrow. You promise you will on conditition that the weather's "a bit poo", as there's a bike meet tomorrow you have to attend. The boys are all texting each other, "Looks like rain, geez. Damn."

Next morning you're up early, twitching the net curtains. "That looks like a crack in the clouds to me – I'm out of here." Into the garage for spot checks, making sure everything is in working order; give the bike a little wipe down; decide which colour leathers to wear. Helmet clean, no scuffs.

Down to the Sunday café to meet up with the boys at about 10am, where one by one everyone's mobile rings. The "other halves" are livid: "But you promised to take me to Ikea!" You explain whilst looking round at the others with That Expression, "I'm really sorry, babe, but the boys need me."

Fabrications out of the way, the crew goes for a "chase" first (B road down to the coast, then up to Box Hill). Four thousand bikes in a car park, their owners stand around and pose. After about an hour, someone makes the move towards the road back to London, pulling off their signature moves, tricks & stunts. Unless, of course, you've attracted a crowd of onlookers, hungry to see something proper. Then a "Secret Location" is selected for an elite audience (don't want to "hot it up" with too many people).

The "May Day Run" is the biggest event in the urban biker's calendar, from Orpington to Hastings, typically involving between 80,000 and 100,000 bikes.

BIG HELMET – SMALL HEAD

Not sure why (because they're slightly uncomfortable to wear even when you're on your bike), but you will come across these guys who you'll never see without a helmet. Whether he's undercover, in a hurry or just bored with his hairline, it must get **hot** in there after a while. Makes you wonder…

mopeds

Familiar? That persistent buzzing sound? "L" plates everywhere; no protective clothing; a noisy little gang of 16 year-olds, not allowed to ride big bikes for a few more years, but can they wait? Could **you** wait?

You may be sitting in your car thinking, "How can a bunch of spotty young hoodlums on 'peds with sewing machine engines and dayglo helmets (some with bunny ears on) be threatening to anyone?"

Before you decide to shout anything derogatory (or start spraying them liberally with mosquito repellent), think about how just "one bite" can ruin your whole day; best to let them zoom off the traffic lights and go about your way?

A 'Ped Boy's Worst Fear? "Road Rash": tarmac and (denim) interfused and woven into skin, needing tweezers (and many hours) to remove before healing can take place.

BMX

Secondary school-age boys on the two-wheeled, five-minute flight to school, pulling extra-long wheelies (I must admit, this has always looked cool – knowing how much balance and practice it takes to make perfect), riding on pavements (irritating and upsetting the majority of pedestrians – how often has an elderly person lost an orange or two off their grocery trolley because some heartless teenage cyclist has swept past them in silent mode?)

These are the junior 'Ped Boys, who, in turn, are replaced by the Big Bike Boys. All are doing the same old peacock show. Is it to impress the ladies? No, it's the testosterone doing its thing again: the Competition. And it involves doing Bunny Hops and Railslides on & off of anything they can find.

Now the thing about riding freely on pavements all the time is to be wary of "Laundry Sunday". Every laundrette in the land is doing bumper business (along with the off-licence, the fast-food outlets and, of course, church). Either plan your route and avoid them, or take it all in as part of your obstacle course. Slalom around the congregation on their way to their cars, then see how many laundry bags (each one at least 3ft off the ground) in a row you can Bunny Hop.

"Oh No! He's failed to clear the last bag... The crash team are removing the frilly knickers from his face as we speak... He's okay, folks... He's okay."

scooters

Until recently, it was a convenient way of getting around town and backstreets, but new laws put a spanner in those works, so your Loud and Whiney engine will now get you unwelcome attention from the Old Bill.

The "new lick" is the Electric Scooter: much quieter than the petrol version, and you can slip into Stealth Mode to sneak past those stripey Astras. Only thing is, they need continuous recharging every few hours, so don't stray too far from home (if you were planning to participate in the Paris–Dakar Rally any time soon, this is probably not the best mode of transport for you). And there's no room on the bodywork for your Favourite Logo stickers.

Yes, the standard "No Engine" scooters look great going downhill, but too much effort everywhere else. They were trendy for a Hot Minute, but now:

"Scooters! Get 'em 'ere, cheaps as chips!!"

Don't you feel used? That you paid £100 for yours not too long ago, and now you can get three for a tenner down East Street Market on a Sunday?

They are kids' toys. What did you expect?

skaters

To most city dwellers their surroundings are drab, unappealing, no big deal. These guys just look at life in a whole 'nother light. Everywhere they go is one big playground: One Big Skatepark.

To me a trip to the shop is just that; for a skater, it is another chance to flex. Out the front door, taking a sniff of the air, recording wind speed, board hits the pavement and he's off! As he rolls down the block, everything except the landscape becomes a blur – it's all about motion, the expression of freedom, the escapism. This "popping out for a bit of air" is another opportunity to go to That Place.

You almost expect there to be a new wave of ex-skater architects and landscape designers, the way they study and analyse the urban territory:

"I'll take my run-up from there, fit in a Switch Kickflip, Ollie onto there, Switch 180° to Five-O along there, down that slope, Grind that kerb. Wonder what's over that wall?"

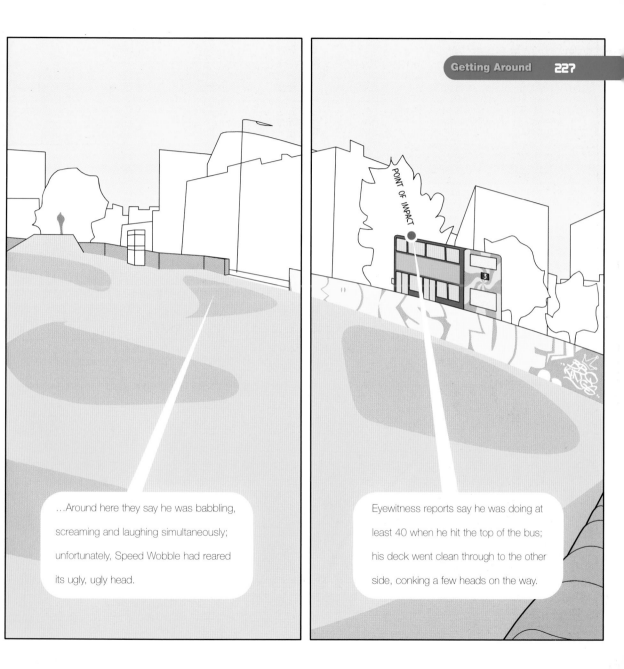

There's also an age-old tribal rivalry between skateboarders and in-line skaters, or rollerbladers – maybe over who has more right to use what patch, what ramps, what park. I'm sure it was the legwarmers over the boots that caused the upset in the first place – "Why don't you go back to disco dancing and leave the tricks to us?"

As for padding, in all of the "Extreme Sports", it's the norm if you are riding professionally, in regular competiton, where there's usually sponsorship, teams and money involved, so safety regulations must be observed. But if you're crawling along the pavement, slower than a sleepy snail, movements severely impeded by a bulky mass of colourful plastic (to accompany your extra-wide and equally-as-garish board, complete with wheels the size of melons), it's not going to gain you an awestruck audience, except to provide canned laughter.

chapter 5
technology

"In the early days, the only people with mobile phones were rich and successful businessmen. And promoters. Despite rumours to the contrary perpetuated by promoters, these are by no means the same thing. Having a mobile was like shorthand for success – it meant you probably had a riverside penthouse and a second Merc in the garage. Then DJs got them – those big old ones the size of an army field. Now everyone's got one – even that homeless geezer who sits by the cashpoint asking for change. Worse still – everyone's on them."

Jaimie D'Cruz, Keo Films

mobile phones

Following the latest fashion doesn't end with clothes, hair and trainers – not by a long shot.

You also have to be up there with James Bond in your knowledge of the latest gadgets. Not necessarily the pocket-watch-mounted, ground-to-air, anti-helicopter, exploding hollow-point tip Chili-Screamer missiles, or the little betting-shop biro with the frog-poison ink, but definitely the extensive area of mobile phones. Technical data, model and chassis numbers, add-ons and plug-ins, Internet compatability, range of ringtones, picture messaging, whether the built-in vibrator is powerful enough for use in foreplay, interchangeable cases, SIM cards, unlocking – the whole shebang must be taken into consideration. And you won't lose any Brownie points for being clued up on the rest: digital cameras, personal organizers, PCs (for making music, or recording and burning your own mix compilation CDs), handheld games. I'm not exactly sure of the relevance of pens with laser sights, though if I was going home one night and was stopped in my tracks by a mass of red dots on my chest, I'd probably fill my shorts – I've seen *Predator* enough times.

Keep up with the pack and you'll be okay; just don't be flashing around your chunky plastic watches with the calculator buttons any more. How often do people really bug you to work out sums for them?

Shifty-looking

"WHAT'S THAT?" I HEAR YOU CRY.
"THERE'S A BLOKE TALKING INTO HIS HAND.
WHAT'S THAT ALL ABOUT THEN?"
YOU'RE TALKING OUT YOUR A**E, MATE!
SOUNDS LIKE SOME FUTURIST SPY SH*T
TO ME.

NEW

WITH THE PATENTED **FINGER AERIAL!**

MICRO-PHONE!!

LITERALLY GOES **INSIDE** YOUR HAND!

WHY?

* FUNKY
* JAZZY
* PETITE
* CONVENIENT
* NOT TESTED
  ON ANIMALS

why not?

* painful installation

* radiation

* ridiculous idea

* not tested on animals

The possibilities are endless. From the Brick to the wafer-thin After Dinner Mint; from the cute to the unnecessarily fancy (there is such a thing as too small – who wants to be constantly searching down the back of the chair for their crisp new toy and finding just crisp? With hair on it?), they are first priority when it comes to showing how "cutting edge" you are. And don't the mobile phone companies know it?

You may have noticed the early age at which the youngsters are becoming hooked on technology. Some of us may remember climbing trees and having hideouts; mudbomb fights and eating toasted sandwiches wrapped in kitchen towel whilst being in goal; seeing how long you could keep a gobstopper in your mouth without crunching it (or cracking a molar)…

I'm sure there are kids out there who'd love to go to the park, approach other kids their own age, football under arm ("Oi, fancy a kickabout?"), or hook up in the treehouse Sunday afternoon for some superhero debate, comics spread out everywhere.

Damn, those are days gone by.

WHAT, IS THAT YOUR NEW MOBILE, SON? HA HA HA!

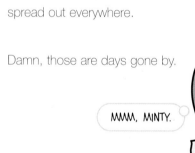

MMM, MINTY.

Now, you've got to remember, if they don't want to speak to you, you will not be spoken to. End of story.

Give off any signal that you're not from the manor, and you will be greeted by blank stares – if you're lucky.

TEXT MESSAGING

Like anything, practice makes perfect. But I see a whole heap of Repetitive Strain Injuries on the horizon (I'm picturing thumbs in bandage on crutches). You have to be able to text as fast as the average person can talk, trust me. Plus you got to be able to keep up with the texting language, the latest abbreviations (the number of times I find myself having to text symbols to my little sister for her to translate them back to me is embarrassing). Sooner or later, schoolteachers are going to have to adapt to the new shorthand.

TALKING IN PUBLIC

An artform, believe. There are two schools of thought here again: being cool and acting like you want to have a private conversation, even politely asking someone to call you back when you'll be indoors; or being so thick-skinned that, regardless of the subject matter, you're happy to broadcast it to the whole world, or shop, or library, or bus. There are also those sad and sneaky few who use their mobile as a prop to weave a web of lies and create a new improved persona to the outside world. You see them out and about, chatting on their phones, wheelin' and dealin' just within earshot of whoever they're trying to impress: girls, peeps, "business associates", etc. Here's an experiment. Next time you see a suspect, when he's not looking, whip the phone out of his/her hand and listen to the caller.

Bet it's the speaking clock or his mum.

YEAH WELL, **BOY**... **RA RA**. Y'**GET** ME?

WE DON'T **ALL** NEED TO KNOW.

TELL HIM AGAIN...

We've all been there. It's evening rush hour. You're on the bus; found yourself a seat next to the window after the mad scramble – "No worries, I ain't getting off for at least an hour. I'll have a little kip."

Then you hear the shrill and cutting sound of electronic, vaguely melodic, UK Garage ringtone. You're thinking, "Please, answer your phone. Please! Look! The bugger's bobbing his head to it! Somebody stop him!!

SOMEBODY STOP HIM!!"

Most of the time these days you'd get away with it, because the general public would rather get home in one piece. ("I saw nothing, I heard nothing, I'm not stressed, work was fine, I love working late, I love being spoken to like a chump…", etc.)

But you can't always bet against your average fellow passenger cracking that evening, with you being the straw that broke the camel's back.

LISTEN 'ERE YOU LITTLE **FREAK**. I'VE HAD JUST ABOUT ENOUGH OF THIS. IF YOU DON'T ANSWER THAT **POXY** PHONE IN THE NEXT FIVE SECONDS, TRUST ME, I'M LOOKING TO TEAR YOUR SCRAWNY HAND CLEAN OFF, **P*SS** ON THE WOUND, THEN TAKE MY BELT AND SCATTER YOUR TEETH WITH THE BUCKLE.

If you're in the phone shop, unsure of tariffs, plug-in-out-WAPs, etc., you can exit with a handful of leaflets and find a park bench to sit on while you try and decipher the small print. Or you can talk to the person behind the till, who (talking very fast) will try and confuse you into buying the most expensive phone with a tariff that only expires on the death of your firstborn and even then can only be terminated by a letter from St Peter himself confirming the decline of your lineage.

A far quicker way is to park yourself behind the coolest looking dude and subtly eavesdrop as HE confuses the salesman into giving HIM a phone for free with all the trimmings. As The Dude leaves and while the salesperson is still spinning, promptly say, "I'll have what he had." Oh, and say it like you mean it. Forget small talk; just leave with your new and very cool phone. (You can read the manual later.)

Remember pagers? Some of the young 'uns won't even have heard of these. Seems they were cool for just a minute – clipped on your belt, on your hip pocket. If you were really "out there", you had one or even two clipped onto your hat. Didn't matter how big they were, it was the fact that you had 'em – that you were so on point people had to be able to find you; any time; day or night! Three little beeps and BAM! You Had To Be Somewhere Else Quick.

But try that now…

the doc says:

Techno jargon is like nuclear physics – you either know about it or you don't. So, if the opportunity arises to have a conversation involving it…

Don't.

OFF ON ONE.

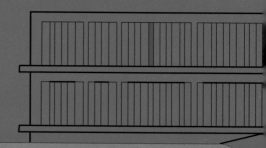

"There are numerous advantages of having a home studio. It is more cost-effective without having to fork out for hire fees and because you are not paying for the time in the studio you can be much more relaxed, more productive and work at your own pace instead of worrying about rushing to finish your productions because you are paying by the hour. But most importantly, the home studio means having the freedom to produce music when you want and how you want!! No one telling you how to or not to. Home studio is all about the freedom factor!!"

DJ EZ (.com)

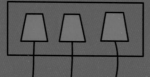

games consoles

You can stop pretending now. Don't worry, this is one pastime you will not be alienated for. This is an area where someone's geeky, trainspotting attention to detail can win friends, props and even a degree of respect under the right circumstances. The hunter can become the hunted; predator can become prey; and the school bully can become the little schoolgirl with ponytails, plaits and braces around teeth. Let the games commence.

Forget what you wanted to watch on the box that night; forget the housework; forget homework; forget the fact that you have a girlfriend/fiancée/wife/mum. She will not understand the necessity of the noise, the need for profanity (and sometimes spitting), the kicking over of drinks on purpose after being knocked out of the competition, the skipping down the hallway screaming after the delivery of that knockout punch – PAPOW!! The crowd goes wild, the loser implodes in the face of your mental and masculine superiority, this is your day. You've waited long enough, and yes, there's a good chance that tonight you will be going without dinner and/or sex, and will be sleeping on the sofa, but wasn't it worth it?

YOU DAMN RIGHT IT WAS!!

Obviously, there are a few drawbacks about this way of life. If you're not careful, you may notice one or more of the following side effects:

* Inability to keep fidgety hands still

* Itchy trigger finger

* Crab Claw (see below)

* Monosyllabic speech (including frequent, violent outbursts; not unlike Tourette's Syndrome)

* General social decline

* Worrying lack of female company

CRAB CLAW

Develops as a result of holding your joypad too tightly, resulting in the involuntary hand clasp and twitchy little finger (these are nasty side-effects but are perfect for gathering bar snacks.)

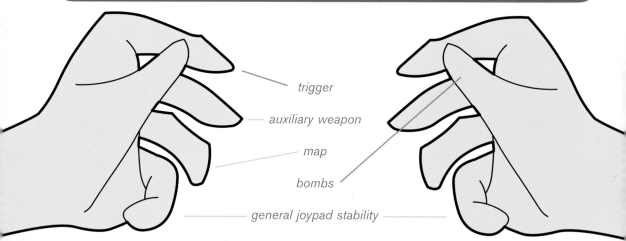

trigger

auxiliary weapon

map

bombs

general joypad stability

Then there's the most worrying aspect of all: the impression we give our young ones – little brothers, sisters and, eventually, our children.

You know what I mean. Look in the video drawer, under the TV, behind certain books in the bookcase. Somewhere in that house, you'll find a still-sweaty console; button markings all worn away from many a night's shooting/driving/tag-team wrestling.

We need to make it clear to the children's minds –

This is NOT exercise.

chapter 6
walking the walk

"My observation throughout the years of clubbing, performing, promoting, etc. is: you meet, you greet, you look and learn and you keep your feet firmly on the ground.

Keep your friends close, but keep your enemies closer!"

Constantine Flowerz, Promoter

By now you should have a good idea of how to rock your gear, from head to toe; how to sport that Finger Wave under your Doo Rag or to spot the equine origin of that suspect weave; how to survive clubbing, funfairs and getting about in general.

All that's left really is the Talking of the Talk AND the Walking of the Walk. Probably the most serious section of the book so far, this involves possible life or death scenarios, where one word will be the difference between smelling of roses and pushing them up. Confidence, arrogance, fear, fearlessness, intelligence, stupidity, or Balls of Steel – any one or a combination of these will earn you stripes for the future. The colour of those stripes is completetely up to you.

Depending on what part of town you're in, you can get a idea of how rough it is by the number of yellow "Can You Help?" noticeboards there are about the place, concentrated in one small area. No two signs say the same thing – there's just not enough pavement space.

You're on the packed evening rush-hour bus as it trundles through the inner city. Commuters on their way home to the suburbs stare out of the windows in disgust at the bleak territory:

"Those poor saps. How can they live like this?"

Well, it's not all bad. Some bright spark made the discovery that the signs made excellent sleds – handrails and everything.

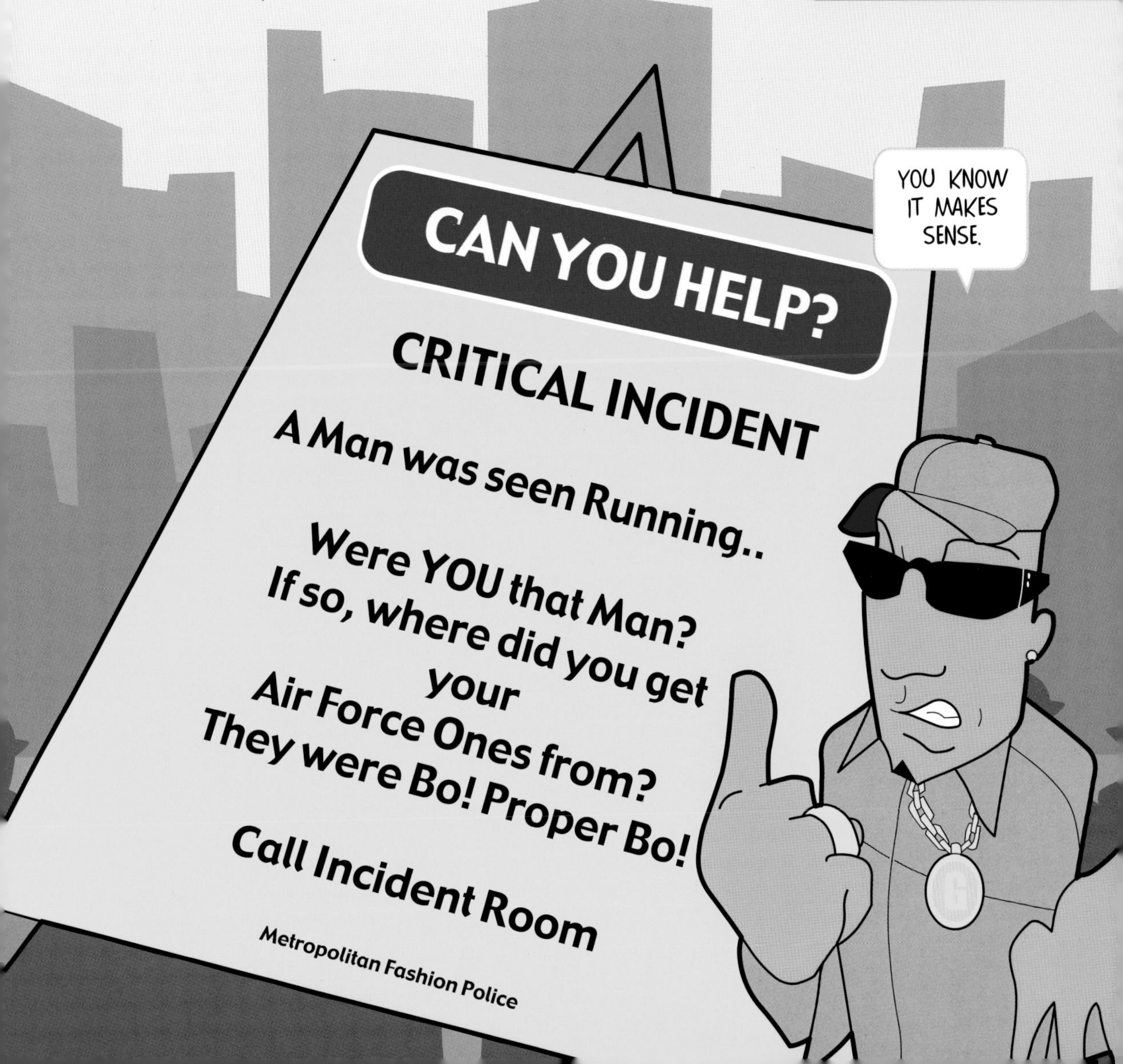
CAN YOU HELP?
CRITICAL INCIDENT
A Man was seen Running..
Were YOU that Man?
If so, where did you get your
Air Force Ones from?
They were Bo! Proper Bo!
Call Incident Room
Metropolitan Fashion Police
YOU KNOW IT MAKES SENSE.

> **"Slang when used right is like morse code for the people. It's how we speak in our real lives."**
>
> Rodney P

slang

Why slang? Well, people have got to have something to call their own, right? As youngsters we develop the habit of forming cliques and tribes, each with its own "isms" and terms. If you want to communicate but not necessarily so that everyone within earshot can understand, the feeling of being included in that small circle of heads that "know the coup" is powerful indeed.

Heavy, dark, cold, hectic, messy, rough, dope, cutting, the Lick, etc:
Bad (meaning good)

Booooo!: Stay on or get off?

Yo, whapp'n, wassup, easy: Hello

Laters, peace out, easy: Goodbye

Seen: I understand

Y'get me?: Do you understand?

Mate, blood, bruv, bredren, geez: Friend

Bling: Jewellery (see pages 92–93)

Bird, skirt, skeet, yattie: Girls

SORRY, WHAT WAS THAT LAST ONE?

"The thing that sets London apart from anywhere else is the cockney rhyming slang! Coming from up North (Notts, you gets!) you listen to people more closely to see what they're on about. After a while, you get the hang of it and **ROBERT'S YA FATHER'S BRUVVA!!** Work it out."

DJ Shortee Blitz

Sight, Sound, You're Havin' a Bubble, Sorted, Sweet, String, Mustard, Gravy, Ruby, Rosie, Brew, Cool Beans, Ya Firm, The Mans, That's Long, That's Minor, Haters, Shotters, Shiners, Stoosh, Stink, Parky, Raggo, Rocky, Rotter, Moose, Minger, Mashed, Caned..

Apples
& Pears?

THE "TOUCH" OR THE "POUND"

You're in a club, at the funfair or even out with your mum shopping and you're pulling the trolley.

You are confronted by a particularly urban-looking chap: can't see all of his face as it's partially covered by a hooded garment or purposely high jacket collar. He's looking or coming in your direction, with one fist raised in front of him. Don't panic and start getting nervous prematurely. More than likely, he's offering you an opportunity to greet him accordingly, by meeting his fist in a similar fashion with your own.

To be on the safe side, just leave your upfacing palm extended, letting him know that you're not from around these parts, not familiar with the customs and therefore would like a simple handshake as a return for his initial offer of friendship.

The mum, having kittens

THE SCREW FACE

"A London club has the highest proportion of Attitude per square inch of any place imaginable. Trance and Hard House are probably your best bet. It's only the gang-like behaviour of the bouncers that will unnerve you. A typical House club is at best a bit pretentious, and is the first place you'll feel you're not good enough to stand in the same room as these people.

Moving into darker realms, a Drum & Bass crowd will soon teach you to keep your head down and your eyes to yourself. Garage is like most of Johannesburg: a No-Go zone for the uninitiated. The streets and the clubs are one, and it's wise not to forget that.

The closer the music is to the Underground, the closer the Underground is to the music and, by proxy, to you. Believe."

Kenton, Kaizen Records

Dry, cracked lips/toothache/lost doorkeys/missed bus/too much pepper

Needs his glasses

Just got dirt on boxfresh white trainers/forgot girlfriend's birthday/diarrhoea

Hayfever – needs a tissue, quick!

Lost Lottery ticket/forgot to defrost the meat/left the oven on/stubbed toe

Painful Trapped Wind

Bought a bad mango/the whole portion of chips were brown/ulcer

Genuinely Hates Everyone & Everything. Did you guess?

your crew

Or your Kru, or your Massive, your Thugs, or Bredrins; Dawgs, Homies,

your Clique, or your Posse.

"I remember how important garms were for your image! Bally Flush, Chipie cords, one leg tucked into your Burlington socks with the little gold button on the side. Nike Flight tracksuit top that you managed to get from a trip to NYC that was so exclusive that you would have to be very careful not to get it 'drapesed' off your back by some ruffneck; and the all-important walk, where you looked like you had one leg longer than the other."

Bru, *Blues & Soul* magazine

the swagger

No running. Unless you're being chased by a big dog, a crackhead on a mission or Old Bill; you walk slow, dragging your feet as you go, giving the impression you've got some hard doo-doo under your arch you're trying to get rid of.

Anyhow.

"What a lovely day. Not a care in the world. Free as a bird. What shall I do with myself? I know – I'll cross to the other side of the road. Why? No real reason, I just feel like it. I'm an unpredictable soul, me. I refuse to be pigeon-holed, caged or cornered. What you see is what you get."

Don't wait for someone to stop their car and let you cross. Just step out freely like you're Unbreakable.

Remember to stare blankly at the driver, who did you the favour by stopping in the first place.

hangin' out

The park playgrounds, youth clubs, pool halls, etc. are slowly but surely being shut down for one reason or another. The kids have got no choice but to hang out on street corners, getting up to every manner of mischief imaginable.

"Two schoolchildren at a time." How easy do you think it is to enforce this? They mill out of school like ants, eager to get to that sugary treasure chest. The shopkeepers dread this part of the day. Of course they'll sell buckets of sweets, crisps and drinks, but with that comes the shouting and the pushing; the numerous sets of fingers feeling up the penny sweets; the fridge door and freezer lid being left open; the complaints of "beady eyes following them around the shop". The list is endless.

When you've finally acquired the taste for alcohol (cheap "paint stripper" wine, Alcopops, your dad's scrumpy, etc.), it's all about trying to get hold of the stuff – most of the gang don't even look their age, so if you're the one with the "whiskers", you're always the one who has to go down the offy.

"Look, star. Just take the money and hurry up. They never grief you for ID, so shoosh your noise."

Then trying to stay out as long as possible to avoid having to face your parents whilst drunk and giggly.

* nasty, vicious, etc.

"WANT SOME, DO YA?"

There are many variations on this theme. Usually a game played out by males of all ages, it starts in the playground at school, then moves on to the streets, the difference here being no referees, playground monitors or childminders to stop that crap before it starts. So, in a nutshell, you're on your own – that is, unless you're part of a "firm" that runs the area or you're properly "tooled up and not afraid to flex".

The main problem with this aspect of the game is that if you lose, you lose royally. Make no mistake – someone's family is about to get that call: either "Mum, bring me some grapes!" or "Mrs Blah-Blah? We'd like you to come and identify a body." Whichever way it goes, it ain't pretty. Therefore the message is simple: Think First. What are the consequences? A particularly fidgety young man sees you and shouts:

"Oi, P***hole! What You Lookin' At?!"

Immediately you have a dilemma. You have to make a quick decision, based on the information available (which is always less than you need, so a good bet is to go with your gut reaction). You may ask yourself, "Who is this guy? He doesn't know me personally and therefore should not be addressing me in this manner," or even, "I don't know this fool, but he don't know me. Why is he so sure of himself that he can just step up and disrespect me? Does he know something I don't? Is he tooled up and high as a kite? Has he got snipers watching me from that tower block?

Is that parked car with the blacked-out windows full of his trigger-happy boys? He's obviously pleased with his odds. The trouble is: am I pleased with mine? Hmmm. I was really looking forward to that footy on the box tonight, but right now I have to teach this fool – no. Forget that. I'm gonna 'low him. I'm starving. Got better things to do. Free it!"

That all happens in the blink of an eye, and yeah, the midget's hailing abuse at the back of your head, but so what? You may never know the outcome of that exchange had you stayed and confronted him (you could have slapped him up and got some enjoyment out of it), but where you are not in complete control of the scenario, you are fully justified in letting it go. In this game the players change daily. You wonder why you don't see certain players any more. That's because they were not enjoying the game as much as they used to, and got out. Or they lost their last battle; now they're out of the game **permanently.**

BRING IT FOOL, I'M FEELIN' LUCKY.

It seems the further away from the city you are, the more likely you are to survive in a scrap. "Good ol' fisticuffs" was the worst part of that faceoff; a black eye, a split lip, a ringing ear – but at least they could laugh about it next week in the pub.

IS THAT THE BEST YOU CAN DO?

male v female

"When you're there, dancing in a club, this guy's been staring at you all night, waiting for you to go over to him. Eventually you decide to go to the ladies', and as you walk past, the guy grabs you by the arm. Is that any way to impress a woman? I've still got marks from where he gripped my arm so tightly."

"The Alcohol Stalker:
He spots you coming into the club, but doesn't have the bottle to speak to you. He gets steadily drunk. Every time you turn around he's there lurking, trying to catch your eye. Finally, he lurches towards you, plastered (passive), gives you the Puppy Dog Eyes, the "please don't blast me" approach;

COME ON LOVE, YOU KNOW I'M MACKING.

I'M DAPPER!

or (aggressive) all up in your face. Way too heavily, spitting drink all over you – a typical conversation always ends with: "F***ing Lesbian!!!" And why is there always a guy who is one of the DJ's entourage, saying, "I can get you in the DJ Box. I can get you drugs. I'll introduce you to the DJ. You're just the sort of girl we need to promote our raves."

Cyd, Clubber

"Me and a friend walked by a group of guys. All you could hear was, "Pssst! Pssst!" So my mate's got fed up with this and turned round to them, shouting, "Is that the sound of your b*lls deflating?!!"

Boogie, MC

> **"Oi – I was in there like swimwear."**
>
> Al Fingers, *DPM Camoflage Book*

THE RUMP RIDERS

These guys congregate at the perimeter of the dancefloor, and see the slightest blink in their direction as an invitation to come and "Ride Your Behind". They're normally harmless, however, and a quick nudge to their nether regions will send them back to their posts, hoping for another chance opportunity. Best not to offend them as this works both ways – by the end of the night even some girls need a Last Resort.

Note: A full hour of this fruity exchange might take place without a single word being uttered (except "No", "Get off", "In your dreams", etc.).

> **"Always have respect for yourself, no matter what others think or say."**
>
> Sabrina, Mis-teeq

YOU MIGHT GET LUCKY

Okay, you've leeched onto that girl for long enough now, the last tune has come and gone. You got butterflies in your stomach, and a little dew on your chest and back – "Will she gimme some program? Can I bear a knockback after all that groundwork?" Remember "Check Yourself" (pages 122–123)? So you did pay attention. It seems your grooming has done the trick. Even though you're clammy with "honest" sweat, so is she – it's all good.

"Alright, come on then. You can stay at mine tonight but I want you out first thing – I got work in the morning."

YEEEEEEE-HAH!!!!!

It's hard to hold it down but you're on your way, squire. The prospect of sex? Carry your own protection – also, check the date on the packaging. Beware of tall, slim women with small bottoms and big feet (especially in a dimly-lit venue). And bringing a toothbrush and flannel rolled up in the lining of your jacket will be noted in the Good Boys Book, getting an "A" for effort.

tripping over in public

...then "styling it out".

NOTHING TO
SEE HERE.

GO BACK
TO YOUR
HOMES.

Walking down the road, when up ahead you notice that "special someone" (who you've had your eye on for a little while now) sitting with a friend in the window of the sandwich bar.

"Damn it, they've seen me! No worries, keep calm. How does my hair stay? Are my jeans mashup? Too late now, they've seen me and they're both smiling – just firm it, look cool and wave."

BUCK! Your Big Toenail nearly comes off with the force.

Ooooh, that's Got To Hurt! The excruciating pain mixed with the embarrassment & shame results in an unbearable cocktail of discomfort. What do you do? You involuntarily break into a light jog (complete with limp) in a crude attempt to convince anyone who saw that you have actually hurt yourself and it wasn't that funny.

GUYS SIT WITH THEIR LEGS WIDE APART

The reasons for this are not anything to do with physical necessity; more as another primal manifestation of the degree of manliness. Though there is a theory that one's "equipment" needs room to breathe (to keep the "plums" cool and so on), most guys would have you believe it's their abnormally-sized "natural gifts" that leave them with no alternative but to sit this way.

Sometimes you'll see two of these "human oddities" trying to share a regular seat on the bus. It ain't easy.

An important point to note: "Gun Fingers", not "James Bond Fingers" (just watch the experts).

"THE REALNESS:

The scene: Mat Ckillz interviews "hardcore" UK emcee on the phone.

Mat Ckillz: Tell me about your lyrics.

Rapper: It's just my lyrics, blood. They're real, you know? I mean, when it comes to spitting, ain't no man can test me, really. It's like when I battle, if a certain man comes at me like a giant, they're gonna leave me like pure embryo, y' get me? See, when it comes to the science of my lyrics, only certain...

Click on phone line.

Mum: Son, your bath is ready.

Rapper: Mum! I'm doing an interview!

Mum: It's just that your bath's ready.

Rapper: Get off the phone, Mum!

Mum: Your bath's going to get cold.

Click.

Rapper: Erm... anyway... what was I saying? Erm, lyrics, right?

It was a bright day when I realized that most UK rappers still live with their Mum – like me."

Mat Ckillz, *Fatboss Magazine*

thug pets

We all understand the need to have a pet. We want to come home from school, college or work to be greeted by that look of excitement and anticipation: wagging tails, over-zealous jumping-up on clothes.

"DOWN, BOY! Ah, you love me though, don't you?"

Anyone who claims they've never ever had that moment of soppiness and enjoyed it is lying to themselves. But when it comes to the pressures of cool, there is No Escape. No more Spot, Fido or Rover; now it has to be Tyson, Snoop or Rizla. The new doggy uniform includes muzzles, chains and harnesses, giving even the most mild-mannered dog the look of a Bondage-club regular.

FEEL LUCKY DO YA?

Staffordshire Bull Terriers, English Bull Terriers, American Pit Bull Terriers; snakes, lizards, scorpions, tarantulas and such, as opposed to budgies and gerbils, rabbits, guinea pigs and goldfish.

Today's dog of choice: American Bulldog.

The '90s: Pit Bull.

The '80s: Rottweiler.

The '70s: Alsatian.

This need for "hard" pets could get silly. What are we to expect next? Portuguese Man-Of-War on a stick? Being waved precariously outside a UKG rave at a crowd of screaming revellers?

"What is it?! It looks like a pic 'n' mix bag!!"
"Oh Sh*t. That's no bag..."

What happened? Winning a goldfish in a bag at the funfair used to be "the lick". What do you really need a piranha for anyway? If you ask me, there is nothing more ferocious than a French Poodle on heat. Don't let the silly haircut fool you.

SH.

> "You have to be a Chameleon. When you live in a big place like London, comprising of many different pockets of people and social groups, you have to be able to communicate and blend with anyone. When Collision is imminent, what you gonna do? Who are you going to be?"
>
> Garfield, Brown Bowler Animation

switching accents

You're used to hearing your Cockney Mechanic mate talking about the Religion of "Boy Racing", whatever. The minute a Rasta randomly passes by the premises…

"Wha'pen Dready – you cool? Yes I, much respect. Hol' it up!"

You're completely dumbfounded, admiring how effortlessly he switches between cockney and Jamaican patois. "What did you just say?" But what isn't good practice is putting on a US accent when you're not American; or speaking in West Indian patois when you have no connection or heritage whatsoever: "He's **Ja-faken**." Think about it.

the old bill

Bull, Babylon, the Rozzers or the Filth – in certain areas talking to them can result in an instant loss of respect. Even something as innocent as asking for directions can undo all your hard work and preparation. Your careless actions can be relayed around the manor in minutes.

"New Boy turn **Informer**."

(and being accused by "Plod" of acting suspiciously in the first place)

> **"Life is a game, and the game is made up of cycles. When the cycle comes round to you, don't disrespect or put people down, because when it's someone else's turn, you might end up regretting it."**
>
> Sticky

having respect

This will save you a whole heap of grief later on down the road. You won't be young and reckless forever. Sooner or later we all have to take responsibility for our actions. So the earlier this brainteaser clicks into place, the easier life becomes.

Having respect for people's parents, no matter how hard you are; having to show decency and manners in the presence of "big people"; that your folks "bring you up good". Think like the Krays: you can be bad as they come, but you treat your old dear like a queen – buying flowers for mums will get you cups of teas made, maybe even slices of cake. You are less likely to be quizzed about your employment status, or ambitions in life – and to get the frown that says, "Right now, your prospects don't look promising."

Coffee Cake and Mrs. Higgs' likeness appears courtesy of Mrs. Anne Higgs.

If visiting someone's house, make sure you have clean socks on. Chances are you may have to leave your shoes by the front door, so as not to distress the people's good carpet (or the highly-polished wooden floors, or the white-as-driven-snow long-haired rug: "What's that? Rice? IS THAT A RICE GRAIN ON MY WHITE RUG??!!!"). And as the majority of city folk live in small homes (you know how it is – millions of people living literally on top of each other; disused land hard to come by; the demolition of schools and other useless buildings to make way for more two-storey, colourful-front-doored housing in attractive cul-de-sac arrangements), imagine being the guilty owner of the smelliest socks, in a compact centrally-heated living room, where the cheesy funk has nowhere to go.

Or the Worst Case Scenario: someone's stepped in fresh doo-doo and has unwittingly scraped the rust-hued remnants EVERYWHERE.

"EEEK! MY RUG!!!!"

If you have only passed by because you were in the neighbourhood, forgot the "No Shoes" rule and you know full well that the way your toes are feeling moist at present, there's no way you're going to let your socks be the One Thing About You That Always Comes Up In Dinner Party Conversation; try this one out:

Shout, "Can I use your bathroom quickly?" and close the door behind you. There's always a good chance there'll be a recently-washed set of smalls on the rack. Grab the driest pair of plain socks you can find, preferably with no distinguishing motifs, and stick those on. Wrap up each of your own sweaties and stuff them into your shoes, to act as a temporary "Stink-Stop". Then, bold as brass, stride confidently into the living room. Your host is none the wiser. You should get away with it "no sweat", unless this person is an obsessive sock-counting freak.

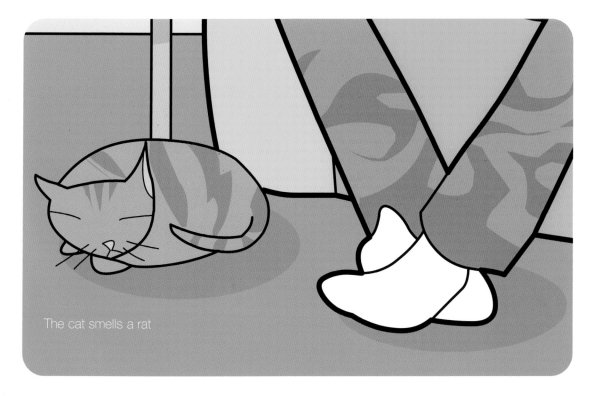

The cat smells a rat

at the cashpoint

Look out for the following:

SHOULDER HAWKING

Someone clocks and takes notes while you're putting in your PIN number. Then after an accomplice distracts you – "Oi mate, you dropped something" – they press "Return Card" and make themselves scarce, with the idea of going for a slap-up meal then shopping – on your behalf.

CARD TRAP

Certain bogus devices are pushed into the slot to stop your card coming back out. Behind you, they watch you put in your PIN, etc., then when you leave the cash machine, they pull out your card and have a field day with your hard-earned "chong".

To minimize the chances of it happening to you, be alert. Have a quick look around you; do not accept amy offers of help from strangers at the cashpoint; and worst come to worst, if it sticks in the cash machine, gets lost or stolen, call up and cancel your card as soon as possible.

beggars

It's like the modern-day version of *Oliver Twist*: kids bunking school to wipe car windscreens at traffic lights – only they're in designer jeans and got new phones hanging out of their back pockets.

It's hard enough to see women roaming the Underground stations clutching babies, but to hear rumours about babies being "borrowed?" To increase the odds of having a good day's begging? Now **that's** disturbing.

The Big City is like "fish in a bucket" to conmen and pickpockets; the pickings are far from slim. The High Street is crowded from the walls to the kerb with shoppers and tourists, a "purse-pincher" is out on a field trip, knife and fork out, napkin around neck – it's feeding time! So protect what's yours: you might be thinking "Bum Bag".

Bum Bag?

If you're on the promenade by the sea – yes. Saturday night out in the city? I should think not. Let us recommend a black shoulder-holster wallet – keeps your "green" close.

TUNNEL OF DEATH?

"Too many wannabe bad boys. Too many guns. Violence is not the answer – creativity is power. The killer is the bassline, or the lyric, or the dance move. We need mental strength and positive thought to survive the Versace Wars"

Johnny Rogue, London 2003

Walking through gangs on your own can be an uncomfortable experience; if you have no alternative, then quick decision-making is the key. Trying to ignore them may not be the best solution:

Are you going to walk around them? Into the road to avoid contact completely? If your sole intention is to "leg it", then you might as well start now – you might be chased; you just might get away.

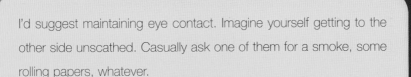

I'd suggest maintaining eye contact. Imagine yourself getting to the other side unscathed. Casually ask one of them for a smoke, some rolling papers, whatever.

Or play the "crazy" card: hum as loud as you can, with a big smile on your face; sing a horribly annoying pop song, gradually increasing the volume the nearer you get; start babbling incoherently, dribble if you have to. Don't ask why – it's just a diversion tactic.

food

There are golden rules and regulations to even the most basic of pastimes, which you ignore at your own risk. Don't say you weren't informed.

Late-night hot dog trolleys

Avoid like the plague – yep, those onions do smell good, but it's the meat you should be worried about.

Kebabs

(Previously covered, pages 162–163.)

West Indian takeaways

There's a very specific way to order food: it's all in the attitude.

Fried (chicken?)

Exactly. How is it those wings are so round?

Chip shops

Your last money, the last portion, the old oil.

Patties

Usually an excellent choice, but check for the date and a make of repute.

Pie & mash

An acquired taste. You may want a taste of the Real London, but come on.

Hot apple pies

Self-explanatory. (Ever been to the earth's core?)

East End bagel shop

Priceless. Fill that post-club belly for less than a fiver.

Spare ribs

Not in front of ladies. Go home, caveman.

Vegetarian

Watch out for anything with spinach (always ends up in teeth) or peas (skins always end up in teeth).

Biscuits

> **"Marks & Spencer: Trouble with the Underwear; but still Strong on the biscuits."**
>
> Will Hobson, Biscuit Don

See how the time of day, plus the amount of alcohol consumed (or level of sanity), affects your choice of food.

The other day I bought myself a midnight snack, and discovered a miscellaneous shape in my Nuggets. What could it have been?

a) a chicken's head

b) a human thumb

c) a human nose

d) Don't even go there...!

money
JOBS

"If you had a choice, would it be to Work or to Play? Mutually exclusive? That's what we're taught! WORK hard at school, get good grades, get a good JOB. Then you'll be able to DO all the things and HAVE all the things that you WANT?? Where's the Play? Oh – at the end of all that WORK! Nah – don't delay the gratification too long, otherwise your life's work will be just that – WORK!!"

Soliheen the Wisechild

What is cool? Should you have to justify an uncool job with the wages you make? For example – **Traffic Warden**: which carries its own risk and stigma, due to the level of hatred directed at them; or **Bike Courier**: also very dangerous, constantly running the gauntlet on two wheels around town. Many teens work in fast-food outlets and are subjected to slave-like working conditions: schoolchildren verbally abusing them, picking up their rubbish from tables and floor, cleaning up discarded food, vomit and such.

CREDIT & HP

All children should have the importance of keeping "good credit" drummed into their heads. The trouble is that we only realize our past mistakes when it's too late – like when you're an adult and you need a mortgage, a family car, the important stuff. Please – don't find out the hard way. Pay off that student loan. Pay off that phone bill. Pay off that catalogue. Believe, the decision to ignore them **will** come back to haunt you. In reality, the Flash Car you acquired on HP (hire purchase) parked outside your mum's house while still living at home; top-of-the-range Home Entertainment System; Titanium laptop; the imported "Lazy Boy" chair?

The day someone realized that if you want something and you don't have the cash readily available you can "buy now, pay later" opened endless "material-possession-acquisition" possibilities. If you want to look the part and be the man, get your mum to put her name down as the creditor. What's the **worst** thing that can happen? Oh, she might get angry when you fail to sort her out with the repayments you promised out of your wages and shout at you. So?

"She knew in the back of her mind that I might fall short on the odd payment when we bought it. What's the big deal?"

You've already endured a lifetime of beating while you were growing up. What else can she throw at you? Go on, have it. What else are mums for?

SIGNING ON

Every couple of weeks another sarcastic Jobsworth "saves your life" by Helping You Back To Work. The supermarket is so grateful to this member of staff for finding you in the Urban Haystack. As you sit there, waiting for "Jobs" to validate your existence – BLING!!!! You spin around. The door flings open. In walks the neighbourhood **SuperFly!** Garms! Jewellery!

Jobs: Can I help you, sir?

SuperFly: **Yeah! I come to sign on!**

Jobs: Do you have your UB40 with you?

SuperFly: **Nah, ain't got it. Just sign me anyway, I'll bring it next time.**

That Guy – how he gets away with it is anyone's guess. How he makes his "wad" is anyone's guess. All I know is, the staff can't stand him, and will do anything to delay his Giro.

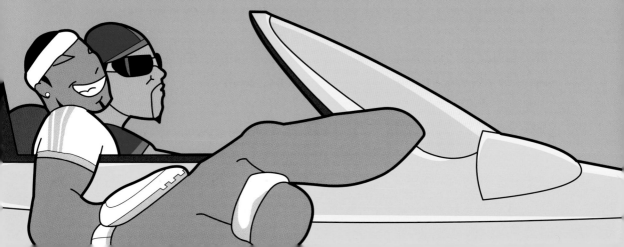

conclusion: judgement night

It had been a long and rocky road, but finally it was the Moment of Truth: Judgement Night. The Doc had given all he could in preparation; his protégé had to step up and be counted. The competition was fierce, but confidence & morale were high. Spent the last week in the Doc's studio: intense vocal training, writing pages of cutting-edge Battle Rhymes. If any of the other MCs wanted to get personal, our hero has been given strict instructions to have none of it. Get Nasty, Get Even, Get the Crowd Involved – once they're on your side, the tide will inevitably turn in your favour.

Clear your mind. It's just you and your opponent. You're not on stage in a hot venue packed with UKG ravers, baying for blood. You're back home "… in a field on your father's land. Standing 50 paces apart facing each other. The smouldering remains of your family home behind you. Cold rain on your face, cold mic in hand. There is No Tomorrow, you've got One Shot…"

The other MCs were flabbergasted. They couldn't get their heads around the fact that this "country boy" was now making them look silly. This guy had lyrics to go, he had attitude, the kid had venom – where the **hell** did he get it from? Then, of course, there was all the female attention he was getting: fluttering eyelashes, kissy faces, folded slips of paper being prepared to be passed to the top dog.

FIRE EXIT

BOOOOOO

"What's the difference between a nice person and a good person?
Anybody can be nice, but the good are hard to find."

Oko, MC